MW00720994

The Definitive Guide for Dog Owners
in Vancouver and the Lower Mainland

MARG MEIKLE

Illustrations by Sa Boothroyd

POLESTAR
BOOK PUBLISHERS

Dog City 🐾 Vancouver

Polestar Book Publishers acknowledges the ongoing support of The Canada
Council, the British Columbia Ministry of Small Business, Tourism and
Culture, and the Department of Canadian Heritage.

Cover photograph by Lionel Trudel
Cover design by Jim Brennan
Printed and bound in Canada

CANADIAN CATALOGUING IN PUBLICATION DATA
Meikle, Margaret, 1956-
        Dog city
        (The city series)
        "Sirius Books."
        ISBN 1-896095-38-0
        1. Dogs—British Columbia—Vancouver—Handbooks, manuals etc. 2.
Dogs—British Columbia—Lower Mainland—Handbooks, manuals, etc. I. Title.
II. Series: The city series (Victoria, B.C.)
SF422.6.C3M44 1997 636.7'009711'33   C97-910809-8

Polestar Book Publishers
P.O. Box 5238, Station B
Victoria, British Columbia
Canada
V8R 6N4
http://mypage.direct.ca/p/polestar/

In the United States:
Polestar Book Publishers
P.O. Box 468
Custer, WA
USA
98240-0468

54321

CONTENTS

*This book is dedicated to
responsible dog owners
and their dogs.*

PREFACE

This is the book Noel and I wanted to buy when we got Rosie, our Border Collie of boundless energy, one rainy winter day. We didn't know where to begin to find out about things doggy, like how to find a trainer or a vet, where you can walk (off leash and on), and what to do with "doo." So I wrote the book, and in the process found out much much more than I expected.

Dogs are hot. If you don't believe me, go to any SPCA, any time, and watch the amount of activity; check out the number of breed clubs and dog associations; or just take a walk in a park. *Dogs in Canada Magazine* says, "one in every four or five families in Canada is living with a dog as a companion, work mate or guardian." That's a lot of dogs, and that's a lot of voters.

Dog folks love their dogs, and love to talk about dogs. Thank goodness. When I started this book I thought I would write small articles on the various subjects I had identified. After many long chats with dog people, I ended up tripling the number of topics, writing a number of articles and reprinting (with permission) a great deal of excellent existing material about local issues. I found that the British Columbia SPCA has an education department brimming with good information. The British Columbia Veterinarian Association and FIDO (Federation of Individuals and Dog Organizations) were very generous, too. It seems like everyone was waiting for someone to do a book like this.

In the end, *Dog City: Vancouver* has turned out to be a resource book for pretty much everything you need to know about owning a dog in the Lower Mainland, from how and where to find a dog, to the nitty gritty of responsible pet ownership, to training, grooming, caring for and showing your dog. Among many things, I found photographers and portrait artists, dog doo extraction companies, dog psychics, how to find an apartment that will take dogs, dog daycares, aromatherapists, programmes for kids and dogs, and dog taxis. And I found plenty of fun. I had no idea, but dog sports have become one of the biggest recreations in the dog world. Every night of the week there are teams of canines leaping hurdles and grabbing balls in flyball practice. There are field, road, den and water trials going on all around us. I had never heard of scent hurdling or Schutzhund training, but now I know who to call to find out about them. To say nothing of dancing with dogs, or "Musical Canine Sports" (a local invention gaining international popularity, and it is something to see!).

I've learned an enormous amount doing this book. I've learned that dog owners are for the most part a very friendly and responsible lot. I've learned that some municipalities are better than others for dog owners who like to exercise their dogs off leash (North Vancouver seems to be the best, Vancouver is currently the worst: no dogs off leash anywhere, any time. See Part IV: Walking Your Dog for insight into the on-leash/off-leash debate). I've also learned that if all dog owners were responsible about controlling their dogs — on and off leash — and about picking up excrement, this would be an easier place to live. If that happened, we could get some more privileges like off-leash park areas and swimming beaches, and there would be a lot more happy non-dog owners out there.

I have tried very hard to get facts straight and be inclusive with *Dog City: Vancouver*. The book is about the whole Lower Mainland of British Columbia — indeed, it ought to be called *Dog City: GVRD* (after the area encompassing the 2,930 square kilometres at the mouth of the Fraser River), but *Dog City: Vancouver* just sounded better. I had to draw the line somewhere, so arbitrarily cut off anything that required a long distance call from Vancouver (although I did make some necessary exceptions). I apologize for any mistakes or people I have missed. Please let me know about these omissions, and if you have any additions, deletions, or comments for the next edition of *Dog City: Vancouver*, please write to me at the address on page 231.

Most of all: I hope this book is as fascinating and informative for you to read as it was for me to write.

— *Marg Meikle, 1997*

ACKNOWLEDGEMENTS

I would like to thank: Bev Atchison, show secretary and enthusiast; Michelle Benjamin of Polestar, for leaping at this project; Joan Bennett, Canadian Kennel Club Director, British Columbia Southwest; Frances Clark, founder of FIDO; J. Cousins, Assistant Supervisor, Animal Control, City Pound; Dr. Adrian Cooper, retired veterinarian; Holly Fitzharding, breeder; Bob Gordon, Vancouver Branch SPCA; Lynn Henry, editor by e-mail; Stephen Huddart and Craig Naherniak of the British Columbia SPCA; Dr. Dennis Jackson, Granville Island Veterinary Clinic; Pam LeGault, FIDO; Noel MacDonald, my supportive husband and Rosie's pal; Maureen Meikle, my mom the fact checker; Ainsley Mills, breeder and host of *All About Pets* on Rogers Cable; Michelle Murphy, researcher/writer; Marion Postgate, trainer and obedience judge; Allan Reznick, *Dogs in Canada Magazine*; Ulrike Radermacher, researcher; Ilona Rule, British Columbia Veterinary Medical Association; Sergeant John Schouten and Sarge, Vancouver Police Department Dog Squad; Noni Sharp, president of FIDO; Hugh Wilson, idea man; and the hundreds and hundreds of other very helpful and supportive people I talked to in the course of writing this book.

On May 23, 1997 at 6:45 p.m. Lionel Trudel took the cover photograph of *Dog City: Vancouver* under characteristically overcast skies. Thanks to the following:

Abi the Border Collie, Anna the Nova Scotia Duck Tolling Retriever, Annabelle the Bichon Frise, Apache the Border X, Archer the Golden Retriever, Asha the Lab Retriever X, Bandit the Wire Fox Terrier, Bear the Rottweiller Lab, Benji the Sheba Inu, Biko the Lab, Bob the Yellow Lab, Boomer the Border Collie Lab X, Briggs the Border Collie, Buster the Lab X, Cadie the Nova Scotia Duck Toller, Charlie the Standard Poodle, Cleo the Dalmatian, Colby the Golden Retriever, Congher the Red Doberman, Cooper the mixed breed, Dahli the Border Collie/Australian Shepherd X, Darby the Australian Shepherd, Delilah the Lab, Dilly the Rottweiller, Diva the Lab X Rottweiller, Eliane the

Bouvier de Flandres, Elijah the Black Lab, Emma the Airedale, Emma the Keeshond, Ferris the Husky X, Flax the German Shepherd puppy, Forest the Lab Border Collie X, Frolic the Golden Retriever, Greyhounds Silver, Lucifer and Vignette, Grimsby the Golden Retriever, Guenther the Harlequin Great Dane, Hadley the Cairn Terrier, Honey the Terrier X, Internet the Border Collie Mix, Iona the Golden Retriever, Ivy and Kemp the Schipperkes, Jessie the Golden Retriever Irish Setter X, Joey the Border Collie, Kira the Shepherd X, Lady the Sheltie, Lucy the Coonhound X, Lucy the Lab X, Lucy the Terrier Mutt, Mardi the Norfolk Terrier, Max the Golden Retriever, Maya the Vizsla X, Meg the Westie, Mika the Alaskan Malamute, Mingus the Black Lab, Muggsie the Black Lab, Odin the Flat Coated Retriever, Otis the mixed breed, Quille the Golden Retriever, Renee the Yellow Lab, Rosie the Border Collie, Rosie the Mastiff, Rusty the Heinz 57, Sabra the Doberman Pinscher, Sally the Pound Dog, Sasha the Dalmatian X, Sam the Border Collie X, Sancho the Portuguese Water Dog, Sarge the German Shepherd, Sergeant Pepper the Miniature Pinscher, Shilo the Golden Retriever, Solange the Golden Retriever, Smoke the Celtic Terrier, Sunday the Yellow Lab, Tanya the mixed breed, Tasha the Shepherd and Lab X, Theo the Shih Tzu, Tia Maria the Chocolate Lab Retriever, Tramp the Border Collie X, Tuppence the Toy Poodle, and the Whippets Saillie, Duchess, Rain and Puzzle. And thanks to all of their owners, too.

INTRODUCTION

Dr. Stanley Coren

Scientists tell us that humans and dogs started living together around 14,000 years ago, which would be about 13,850 years before the City of Vancouver appeared on a map. The first European dogs that came to Vancouver may well have been the two great Mastiffs that the British explorer, Captain George Vancouver, brought with him when he navigated through the Pacific Northwest in 1798. Vancouver's dogs were not the first dogs in the region, however, since many of the Aboriginal tribes in the region also kept dogs. The Native dogs were not used for hunting but rather were used as draught animals for the hauling of goods. There were also special dogs grown for their fur. "So compact were their fleeces that large portions could be lifted up by a corner without causing any separation," according to Vancouver. This dog hair was pounded into felt which was then used for making blankets and clothing. The coming of the Europeans was inauspicious for the Native dogs. The "transport dog" lost its job to the more efficient horse, while the "wool dog" was put out of business by the Hudson's Bay Company's mass-produced trade blankets. That's the way it has always been for dogs in the Vancouver area: Sometimes they are looked after and cherished for who they are and what they can do; at other times they are spurned or ignored.

At first blush, the natural settings in Vancouver would seem to provide the ideal environment for dogs. In the city — or just a short distance away — there are beaches to walk, parks to stroll through, mountains to climb and woods to explore. However, the dog owner must be careful, since not all venues in the Vancouver region are dog-friendly. Indeed, Vancouver residents show a broad range of feelings toward canines. There are many residents who feel that God demonstrated love for humans by giving us the dog as a companion and helpmate, and that life without a dog would be too grim to bear. There are others in this city who believe that dogs were banished from the Garden of Eden for committing the first public nuisance in what had been an unblemished paradise. These conflicting attitudes toward dogs reflect the myriad of different cultural and social influences in this changing city. Still, despite the conflicting feelings about canine companions, there are many dogs in the city. Some recent estimates suggest that one out of every five families in the Vancouver area lives with a dog.

Given that there are so many dogs in the region, one might expect that there would be many resources available to make the lives of dogs and their masters more pleasant — and this, in fact, is true. Yet it is also true that many of Vancouver's dog owners do not know where to find the resources to fill their dog's needs, whether for basic things such as emergency medical care, grooming, training and socializing with other dogs, or for more esoteric matters such as breed clubs, dog shows, dog sports and dog-related recreational activities. Knowledge of these resources is often passed on by word of mouth — and then only if you are lucky enough to know someone who is in touch with the local "doggy world."

Fortunately, Marg Meikle, the author of this book, has provided you with an organized guide to dog information. Marg gave up the chance to become a full-time academic researcher in order to find answers to the questions of ordinary people, and even earned the title of "The Answer Lady" from her numerous radio appearances on the CBC, where she provided listeners with hidden gems of information. Marg has now tried to answer the important question for all of us who love dogs in Vancouver: How to get the best out of life with your dog in and around the city. In the course of doing so, she has spoken to dozens of people associated with the "doggy world" in the city. Gathering all of this useful material for the dog owner has not always been easy. Sometimes, she tells me, it has been quite rough — or did she say "rough, rough"? No matter how daunting the task, the end result deserves our admiration. This first-ever guide to the dog world in the Vancouver area should improve the quality of life for all dogs and dog owners — and therefore for all citizens — in and around the City of Vancouver.

I. Finding Your Dog

So you have decided you want to own a dog. Well, be warned that finding the dog to suit you and your family takes some work! This chapter is about research, research, research, all of which will pay off hugely in the long run. Here are the big questions: Should you really get a dog? What kind of dog should you look for? And where do you get it? Reading, talking to people and working through the Society for Prevention of Cruelty to Animals (SPCA) checklist is a good start. As well, visit dog shows, chat with dog owners galore and use the services of breed clubs, shelters and animal welfare organizations. All of this will make you confident that your constant companion is the perfect match.

BEFORE ADOPTING

Do You Want a Dog, or Do You Want This Dog?

It is a simple idea: The most important visit to a veterinarian is the visit *before* you get a dog. Book an appointment to talk about your personality, how active you are, where you live, how much you like your garden, how many people you live with and what they like to do. The vet will recommend dogs that suit your lifestyle, discuss the virtues of puppies and older dogs, and advise you on how to find that perfect dog. Dr. Adrian Cooper, a retired veterinarian, says that vets love it when people come in for this sort of appointment because they become part of making a good match between owners and dogs. The vet will be in on your new relationship from the beginning — and that's a good thing.

Things to Consider About Adopting a Dog

— *British Columbia SPCA*

1. Why do you want a dog?
It's amazing how many people fail to ask themselves this question before they get a pet. Adopting a dog just because it's the thing to do or because the kids have been pining for a puppy is usually a big mistake. Don't forget that pets may be with you 10, 15, even 20 years.

2. Do you have time for a dog?
Dogs — along with cats, and other animal companions — cannot be ignored just because you're tired or busy. They require food, water, exercise, care and companionship every day of every year. Many animals in the shelter are there because their owners didn't realize how much time it took to properly care for them.

3. Can you afford a dog?
The monetary cost of dog ownership can be quite high. Licenses, training classes, spaying and neutering, veterinary care, grooming, toys, food and other expenses add up quickly.

4. Are you prepared to deal with special problems that only a dog can cause?

Flea infestations, scratched-up furniture, accidents from dogs that aren't yet housebroken and unexpected medical emergencies are unfortunate but common problems that come with dog ownership.

5. Can you have a dog where you live?

Many rental communities don't allow pets, and most of the rest have other restrictions. Make sure you know what they are before you bring a dog home.

6. Is it a good time for you to adopt a dog?

If you have kids under six years old, for instance, you might consider waiting a few years before you adopt. Problem-free pet ownership requires children who are mature enough to be responsible. If you're a student, in the military, or travel frequently as part of your work, waiting until you settle down is a wise choice.

Photograph by
K.A. Davidson

7. Do you know who will care for your dog while you are away on vacation?

You'll need either reliable friends and neighbours, or money to pay for a boarding kennel or dog-sitting service.

8. Will you be a responsible dog owner?

Having your dog spayed or neutered, obeying community leash and licensing laws, and keeping identification tags on your dog are all part of being a responsible dog owner. Of course, giving your pet love, companionship, exercise, a healthy diet and regular veterinary care are other essentials.

"Ah! you should keep dogs — fine animals — sagacious creatures!"

— Charles Dickens,
The Pickwick Papers

9. Finally, are you prepared to keep and care for the dog for its entire life?

Remember: When you adopt a dog, you are making a commitment to care for the animal for its lifetime.

Course on Finding a Dog

Through North Shore Continuing Education, behaviourist Ann Jackson teaches a course called "Considering a Puppy for the Family." She covers choosing the best puppy for your family; breeds and temperaments; preparing your home for the arrival; and helping your puppy form good habits from the first day. The course also includes an introduction to motivational training. She encourages children over 10 years old to attend too. Call 986-8888 for more information.

WHERE TO LOOK

Where Do You Find Your Ideal Dog?

— Canadian Veterinary Medical Association

When you go searching for your ideal dog there are several places you should look. Animal shelters often have a wide variety of dogs in their kennels. Many dogs end up in shelters through no fault of their own and it is wrong to assume they won't make ideal pets. They may have been abandoned and just need a second chance at a loving home.

Painting by
Elaine Sills

If you have your heart set on a purebred dog, consult the Canadian Kennel Club (CKC). The CKC is incorporated under the *Animal Pedigree Act*, a federal statute. One of the objectives of the CKC is to maintain a system of registration of purebred dogs that satisfies the requirements of the *Animal Pedigree Act*, Agriculture Canada and the club members. You should buy purebred dogs directly from a reputable breeder. A veterinarian, the *Dogs in Canada* annual directory, or a breed club (see "Breed Clubs" below) should be able to direct you to a reputable breeder.

Once you find a breeder, you should always inspect the facilities and the dogs yourself. You should also ask for references from satisfied owners. A reputable breeder will ask you questions to ensure you will provide a good home for the dog. A good breeder will have their breeding stock checked and certified against genetic disorders and will sell puppies with at least one set of vaccinations, a non-breeding agreement and a guarantee against genetic disorders. Beware of breeders who will not allow you to see their kennel facilities and at least one parent of the puppy, or who breed a large number of breeds.

Buy your dog only with the approval of your vet. Set up your appointments so that you see the dog and take it directly to the vet's office for a pre-purchase exam. Don't take it home first — this is a sure step towards you keeping it, no matter what the existing or potential problems.

Another place to look for a dog is at a pet store. Some pet stores sell puppies, while others serve as adoption agencies, matching prospective owners with dogs from animal shelters. If the puppies are not from an animal shelter, ask the pet store owner for information about the breeder before selecting a puppy. Look for the same qualities in a pet store as you would in a dog breeder's facility. Good pet stores and dog-breeding facilities should boast clean living areas, knowledgeable staff and healthy-looking pups. Expect a breeder or store staff to talk frankly about the nature of the animal you have in mind.

In Canada, there is a growing awareness of the existence of puppy mills. Mills produce large numbers of puppies in poor, unhygienic conditions. Puppies raised in mills are often unsociable and make unsuitable pets. More important, conditions in mills are often unhealthy and the breeding dogs and puppies in them live unhappy lives. Be wary of buying a dog from someone who won't or can't tell you where the dog was born and raised. You should contact the Society for the Prevention of Cruelty to Animals (SPCA) or local humane society to report an establishment selling obviously unhealthy dogs.

There are regulations and by-laws governing the exchange and acquisition of registered purebred dogs, and it is worth fully investigating these rules before you set out to find your dog. For instance, when a dog is sold as purebred for compensation (monetary or otherwise), the person selling the dog must, within six months of the sale, provide the new owner with a Canadian certificate of registration which records the change of ownership. Alternatively, if the dog is registered somewhere other than Canada, or if the new owner does not intend to register the dog in Canada, this must be formally noted. It is also the responsibility of the person selling the dog to complete all necessary forms and pay all fees, as required by the CKC by-laws.

Whether you look for your dog at an animal shelter, a dog breeder's facility or a pet store, be sure to ask questions about each individual dog. The staff may have noticed certain behaviour and traits in either the dog you are considering or in its parents. If it is possible, try to see the dog's parents, since they may display desirable or undesirable traits not yet evident in their offspring. If you adopt the dog from an animal shelter, ask the staff if they have noticed anything, good or bad, about the dog's behaviour. Some animal shelters conduct temperament testing of the dogs they have available for adoption.

Recommended Reading

Dr. Adrian Cooper is a retired veterinarian and a media spokesperson. These are his favourite books on finding a dog:

Second Hand Dog, by Carol Lea Benjamin (Howell Books)

The Perfect Puppy: How to choose your Dog by its Behaviour, by Benjamin and Lynette Hart (W.H. Freeman and Company)

Lori Staehling is a dog trainer and the owner of two Golden Retrievers, Ginger and Teddy. Her favourite books on finding a dog are:

The Perfect Match, by Chris Walkowicz (Howell Book House)

Choosing a Dog (Your Guide to Picking the Perfect Breed), by Nancy Baer and Steve Duno (Berkley Publishers Group)

Allan Reznik, editor of *Dogs in Canada Annual* (the under $10 bible for anyone looking for a dog, found at newsstands and pet stores) recommends our very own "made in Canada" book on dog selection and care:

The Canadian Dog Owner's Companion: A Guide to Selecting, Caring for and Training Your New Dog or Puppy, by Donna Davidson and Penny Manning (Macmillan Canada).

When you get a dog from any source, be sure to reach an agreement about returning it. You should be allowed time to take the animal to a veterinarian of your choice for an examination to ensure it is in good health. If you are offered a guarantee, make sure you understand exactly what the guarantee means for you and your dog.

PUREBRED DOGS

Tips on Finding Purebred Dogs

Here are some tips about adopting a purebred dog: Read everything you can about breed characteristics, and keep in mind the purposes for which these dogs were originally bred (see the CKC list below). If you are considering buying a purebred dog from a petshop, please read pages 16 to 17 above.

In the Lower Mainland, the best opportunity to see all the breeds of dogs you have been reading about is the annual Lower Mainland Dog Fanciers of British Columbia show. It takes place in October at the Abbotsford Tradex and is the largest such show in Canada. If they aren't busy, most of the exhibitors are very approachable and knowledgeable about their breeds. At the very least, you can gather business cards so that you can go and visit their establishments later. And watch the competitions — they are fascinating.

Breed rescue is another way to find a purebred dog. Dogs end up in rescue through no fault of their own. An owner might have died or become incapacitated, or may have had to move overseas or across country; a new baby might have arrived; or owners may have re-thought the commitment of pet ownership. If a dog has been abused, much care must be taken before placing it again.

Greyhound Rescue is the most well-known type of breed rescue. Greyhound Air's ads feature a rescue Greyhound. There is no Greyhound racing in Canada, but a large gambling operation exists in the United States. Dogs that can't race — for any number of reasons that don't affect the worthiness of the dog as a family pet — are disposed of. Through Greyhound Rescue, more than 8,000 Greyhounds were placed in homes throughout North America last year. Over the past five years, about 200 such dogs have been placed in British Columbia, through June Harrison and five other volunteers of the Greyhound Club of Canada (local chapter), and through the Seattle chapter of Greyhound Pets of America.

For more information on rescue, contact the club for the breed in which you are interested.

A pedigree is simply a genealogical table showing the ancestral line of descent of a registered dog.

"Papers" means more than a pedigree. It is illegal to sell dogs as purebred unless the seller confirms the registration papers. "Purebred" means a dog that is registered, or eligible for registration, with the Canadian Kennel Club (i.e. must be on the list of recognized breeds).

Breed Clubs

The Canadian Kennel Club doesn't sanction Breed Clubs, but they do "recognize" them. Breed Clubs need to meet certain guidelines to maintain recognition and only recognized clubs can hold CKC-approved events.

There are several types of clubs in both specialty and all-breed categories. Specialty clubs can be National (of which only one for each breed can exist), Regional or Provincial, and Local. Recognized specialty clubs can host a spectrum of official events (for the breed or breeds for which they are recognized to promote) such as conformation trials, obedience, field trials, lure coursing and tracking. Specialty clubs also exist to promote a breed, and many have their own newsletters as well as published material on the pros and cons of their breed. Many clubs are involved at some level with Rescue (see above) and can lead you to reputable breeders if you are looking for a puppy. Many also hold fun days such as breed walks or picnics so that members and the interested public can get to know other people involved with the same breed of dog.

All-breed clubs (clubs that promote more than one breed) are permitted to hold all-breed events for conformation and obedience. These clubs usually operate within a radius of approximately 25 miles from a given point. In other words, all-breed clubs are localized.

The Canadian Kennel Club is incorporated under the Animal Pedigree Act (which is a federal statute). One of the objects of the CKC is maintaining a system of registration of purebred dogs that satisfies the requirements of the Animal Pedigree Act, Agriculture Canada and the Club members. Canada is the only country in the world where pedigrees are backed by the federal government.

The assignment: a breeder's business card that would show how easy it is to handle Airedales. The result: four dogs sat still in a canoe as the breeder paddled back and forth for re-takes. Well-behaved indeed!

Photograph by Wendy Wedge

Q: Why did the dog put
on a sweater?

A: It was a chilly dog.

The Bassett Hound Walk is
on the 1st Sunday in May,
rain or shine. It was the
original Vancouver Dog
Walk.

Specialty Clubs (alphabetical by breed):

Airedale Terrier Club of Canada
Pip Smith
924-2083

Akita Action Association
Rosemary Woodworth
922-7914
Newsletter: *Akita Connections*

Akita Club of BC
Lee Oiom
588-0280
Newsletter: *Akita Club of BC Newsmagazine*

Alaskan Malamute Club of Canada
Sandy Logan
Box 7, Site 2, R.R. 1
Cochrane, Alberta
TOL OWO

Australian Cattle Dog Club of Canada
Violet Tipping
795-7788
Newsletter: *Heeler Holler*

Australian Shepherd Club of BC
Airlie Ogilvie
266-4206
website: http://www.australian-shepherds.bc.ca
Newsletter: *Northern Notes*

Bassett Hound Club of BC
Bonnie Tetlock
522-5366
Newsletter: *Scoop*

Beagle Club
Jan Jeske
888-4205
website: http://www.geocities.com/Heartland/Hills/
3441/
Newsletter: *The Bugle*

Bearded Collie Club of Canada
Yvonne Poole
22 Juniper Cres.
Unionville, Ontario
L3R 3Z7
(905) 477-7414

Belgian Sheepdog Club of Canada, Pacific Section
Kelley Laan
463-3551
Newsletter: *Belgian Sheepdog Club of Canada*

Bernese Mountain Dog Club of Canada
Coral S. Denis
R.R. 3
Ladysmith, British Columbia
VOR 2EO
(250) 245-3064

Bichon Frise Club of Canada
Garda Johnstone
980-4967

Canadian Bloodhound Club
Brent Davies
514-699-8396

Border Collie Club of Canada
Kimberley Plummer
R.R. 5, Site 32, Box 23
Prince Albert, Saskatchewan
S6V 5R3
(306) 763-1974
e-mail: plumk@sasknet.sk.ca

BC Bouvier Des Flandres Club
Sue Brace
469-2620

A Breeder is responsible for a dog from the day it is born until the day it dies.

Q: Why is a bloodhound like a rose?

A: They both smell good.

Borzoi Canada
Judy Carleton
Box 248
Black Falls, Alberta
TOM OJO
(403) 885-4314

Boston Terrier Club of Canada
Doreen B. Jones
7127 5th St. SW
Calgary, Alberta
T2V 1B2
(403) 259-3295

Q: Which dogs are the world's best prizefighters?

A: The Boxer and the Doberman puncher.

Dogwood Boxer Club
Monika Pinsker
882-1490
Newsletter: *Tattle Tails*

Western Canada Boxer Club
Sheila Verhulst
530-1389
This is the oldest booster club in Canada, started in 1945.

Canadian Briard Club
Judy Benson-Jones
57 Hilton Ave.
Toronto, Ontario
M5R 3E5
(416) 536-2555

BC Brittany Spaniel Club
Carl Meadows
462-8886

Q: What dog is similar to a cow?

A: A bulldog.

Bull Dog Club of America
Carol Hibbert
420-6053

Bull Mastiff Fanciers of Canada, BC Chapter
Sylvia Lawton
531-3895

Bull Terrier Club Of Canada, BC Division
Debbie Francis
929-7202
Newsletter: *Bull Courier*

Cairn Terrier Club of Canada
Glenn Sergius
522-6362

Canadian Cardigan Corgi Club
Shelley Camm
11722 Mississauga Rd., RR4
Georgetown, Ontario
L7G 4S7

Cavalier King Charles Spaniels of BC
Brigitte Falch
462-1087
Newsletter: *Cavalier Chronicles*

Chihuahua Club of BC
Edna St. Hilaire
521-0922
Newsletter: *The Long and the Short of It*

Chinese Shar-Pei Club of Canada
Rhonda Harvey
31 Waterfield Dr.
Scarborough, Ontario
M1P 3W6

Chow Chow Fanciers of Canada
Suzanne Staines
826-3284

Clumber Spaniel Club of Canada
Sue Grant
18 McCormick St.
Welland, Ontario
L3C 4L9

Glenn Sergius, a cairn terrier breeder and well-respected dog expert, leads annual tours to the Crufts Dog Show in England each March. In June of 1998 he will lead a trip to the World Dog Show in Helsinki. Call for further information: 522-6362

BC Cocker Spaniel Club
Francine Glazer
532-0351
Newsletter: *Cocker Tales*

Collie Club of BC
Sandy MacFarlane
530-7551
Newsletter: *The Collie Classic*

Western Dachshund Club
Susan Lankau
943-4304
e-mail: Slankau@axionet.com
Newsletter: *The Badger Hound News*

Dalmatian Club of Canada
Betty Piers
597-2856

Dandie Dinmont Terrier Club of Canada
Ms. M. Macbeth
Graymalkin Manor, R.R. 3
Stouffville, Ontario
L4A 7X4

Doberman Pinscher Club of BC
Cynthia Lerfold
576-8809
Newsletter: *Dobie Drumbeat*

English Cocker Spaniel Club of Canada
Linda Beason
1317 White Rd.
R.R.2, Site G, C-30
Nanaimo, British Columbia
V9R 5K2
(250) 722-2912

BC English Springer Spaniel Club
Dorothy Hunchak
596-4063

"Cynography" means the history of the dog.

"Cynegetics" is the art of training and hunting with dogs.

"Cynorexia," or an appetite like that of a dog, is used to describe insatiable hunger.

Flat Coated Retriever Society of Canada
Kathy Condrat
824-1090

Western Gazehound Club
June Beard
532-7032
Formed to promote the 10 Gazehound breeds: Afghan Hounds, Basenjis, Borzoi, Deerhounds (Scottish), Greyhounds, Ibizan Hounds, Irish Wolfhounds, Pharaoh Hounds, Salukis, Whippets.

German Shepherd Dog Club of BC
Ona Steffensen
534-2344

Golden Retriever Club of BC
878-GOLD
Newsletter: *Golden Tails*

Gordon Setter Club of BC
Barbara Young
538-6111

Western Great Dane Club of BC
Gail Demers
856-3378
Newsletter: *Western Great Dane Club of BC Newsletter*

Westcoast Great Pyrenees Association
Pat Moore
943-0942
Newsletter: *Westcoast Pyrspectives*

Group V Dog Club of BC (All of the Toy Breeds)
Lynn Weir
594-1535

Group VI Specialty Club of BC
Bonnie Hubert
931-6458

Relief sculpture by Steve Hall

Temperament Testing is a useful tool for testing your dog's soundness for behaving in society, and looks at stability, provocation, socialization. The Westcoast Great Pyrenees Association often holds clinics.

There's a guy with a Doberman Pinscher and a guy with a Chihuahua. The guy with the Doberman says to the guy with the Chihuahua, "Let's go over to that restaurant and get something to eat." The guy with the Chihuahua says, "We can't go in there. We've got dogs with us." The guy with the Doberman replies, "Just follow my lead." So they walk over to the restaurant and the guy with the Doberman puts on a pair of dark glasses and walks in. The doorman says, "Sorry, no pets allowed." The guy with the Doberman says, "You don't understand. This is my seeing-eye dog." The doorman says, "A Doberman ?" The owner replies, "Yes, they're using them now, they're very good." So the doorman says, "Come on in."

The owner of the Chihuahua figures, "What the hell!" So he puts on a pair of dark glasses and walks in. The doorman says, "Sorry, pal, no pets allowed." The guy with the Chihuahua says, "You don't understand. This is my seeing-eye dog." The doorman says, "A Chihuahua?" The guy with the Chihuahua exclaims, "You mean they gave me a Chihuahua?"

Greyhound Club of Canada
Ann Webster
856-2850
Newsletter: *Greyhound Club of Canada*

Irish Setter Club of BC
Pam Legault
856-1496
Newsletter: *Redhead Review*

Irish Terrier Club of Canada
Sue Cairns
924-0414

Irish Wolfhound Club of Canada
Emma Ross-Awde
820-8273

Italian Greyground Club of Canada
Kathy Crane
3959 St. Margarets Bay Rd.
Hubley, Nova Scotia
B3Z 1C2

Pacific Jack Russell Terrier Club of BC
Lois Clough
536-2401

Keeshond Club of BC
Ron Purvis
820-0282
Newsletter: *Kees Expressions*

Western Canada Kerry Blue Terrier Club
Leone Templeton
325-3157
Newsletter: *Kerry-Go-Round* and *Kerry Clips*

Kuvasz Club of Canada
Dorothy Grosart
72 Bythia St.
Orangeville, Ontario
L9W 2S5

Lhasa Apso Canada, BC Branch
Arlene Miller
929-3570

Lowchen Club of Canada
Janey LaPointe
S7A, C29, R.R. 4
Vernon, British Columbia
V1T 6L7

Miniature Pinscher Club of Canada
Carol Swan Lang
855-1720

Newfoundland Dog Club of Canada, BC Region
Denise Castonguay
462-7231
Newsletter: *Newfsletter*

Norwegian Elkhound Club of BC
Donna Surman
435-3213

Nova Scotia Duck Tolling Retriever Club of Canada
Andrea Mills
467-3576

Western Canada Pekingese Club
Margaret Roberge
929-2192

American Pit Bull Terrier Association of BC
Ellen Nordstrom
856-6417

Poodle Specialty Club of BC
Carol Swan Lang
855-1720
Newsletter: *Poodle Patter*

"Poodles always listen attentively when being scolded, looking innocent, bewildered and misunderstood."
— James Thurber

Photograph by David Beckett

Portuguese Water Dog Club of BC
Debra Barcon
535-4979
Newsletter: *Tide Lines*

Pug Dog Club of BC
Ruth Modder
543-9180
Newsletter: *Pug Pause*
websites: http://www.camme.ac.be/%7Ecammess/
www-pug/home.html
http://www.compupets.com/lmdf/pug.htm#top

BC All Retriever Club
Cathy Tweeddale
298-7129
e-mail: duckndog@dowco.com
Newsletter: *BC ARC News*

Rhodesian Ridgeback Club of Western Canada
Kristine Nielson
534-4786

Fraser Valley Rottweiller Club
Suzanne Elkanger
856-7397

Schipperke Club of Canada
Bonnie Ritchie
533-0014

Giant Schnauzer Club of Canada
Nola Keay
533-8744

Miniature Schnauzer Club of BC
Ken Allen
576-8774

**Standard Schnauzer Club of Canada,
Western Division**
Heather Pedersen
597-0818

Canadian Scottish Terrier Club
Marge Bauer
533-4510

Sealyham Terrier Club of Canada
Bev Atchison
856-8017
e-mail: beva@siwash.bc.ca
Newsletter: *Sealyham Sentinel*

Shetland Sheepdog Club of BC
Brenda Foster
583-9295
website: http://www.compupets.com/sscbc/
index.html

Shih Tzu
see the Group VI Specialty Club of BC
Bonnie Hubert
931-6458

BC Siberian Husky Club
Mimi Kurz
530-0064

Smooth Fox Terrier Club of Canada
Trish Schmidt
Box 205
Wilcox, Saskatchewan
SOG 5EO

Staffordshire Bull Terrier Club of Canada
Belle Campeau
R.R. 1, 2133 County Rd. 20
Oxford Station, Ontario
KOG 1TO

British Columbia All Terrier Club
Bev Atchison
856-8017
e-mail: beva@siwash.bc.ca
Newsletter: *Terrier Times*

"Just because someone is a member of the Canadian Kennel Club doesn't mean he won't sell you a purebred puppy with potential problems. A good breeder will always offer a written guarantee."
— Marion Postgate, trainer, instructor, Schipperke breeder

Tibetan Terrier Club of Canada
Terry Gueck
944-2014

Tibetan Spaniel Club of Canada
Barbara McConnell/May McConnell
857-4656
Newsletter: *Tibetan Spaniel Club of Canada Newsletter*

Photograph by
David Beckett

Vizsla Canada
Glen Way
(250) 385-3238
Victoria

Weimaraner Association of Canada
Wendy McKay
4883 Torbolton Ridge Rd., R.R. 2
Woodlawn, Ontario
KOA 3MO

Welsh Terrier Association of Canada
Jennifer Weeks
85 Royal York Blvd.
Sault Ste. Marie, Ontario
P6A 6X3

Soft Coated Wheaten Terrier Association of Canada, BC Section
John Rogers
583-2456
Newsletter: *Soft Talk*

BC Whippet Racing Club
Lorna Leinback
536-0484

Lower Mainland Whippet Association
Bonnie Goebel
856-4763
Newsletter: *Rabbit Habit*

Whippet Club of BC
June Harrison
574-5786

White Shepherd Club of Canada
Elaine Twanow
826-0641

Wire Fox Terrier Club of Canada
(250) 595-2889

All-breed Clubs:

Auld Land Syne Society
Monika Pinsker
882-1490

Fraser Valley Dog Fanciers Club
Bonni Patterson
576-9774

The Lower Mainland Dog Fanciers of BC
Sylvia Lawton
531-3895
website: http://www.compupets.com/lmdf

Mission Kennel Club of BC
Carol Tracy
530-0501

Oceanside Kennel Club
Joyce Ann Moulton
574-7101

Pacific Kennel Club
Leona Palylyk
535-8071
website: http://www.alphagate.com/pkc/

Renaissance Dog Association
Monika Pinsker
882-1490

Photograph by
Kent Southwell

Richmond Dog Fanciers
Lil Geddes
241-0705

Ladies Kennel Club of British Columbia
Sheila Verhulst
530-1389

Western Federation of Individuals And Dog Organizations (FIDO)
volunteers: 681-1929 / 277-3158 (emergency only)
fax: 277-4285

Elsie Murray Canine Centre Society
Sheila Verhulst
530-1389

Breeds Recognized by the Canadian Kennel Club

— Dogs in Canada Annual

For purposes of conformation showing, the Canadian Kennel Club categorizes its recognized breeds into seven groups, based chiefly on their original function, as summarized below. In addition, the CKC has more than 140 breeds in its Miscellaneous class, a "staging area" for full recognition.

Group 1 — Sporting Dogs
Bred to point, flush and retrieve game
Braque Francaise
Griffon (Wire-haired Pointing)
Pointer
Pointer (German Long-haired)
Pointer (German Short-haired)
Pointer (German Wire-haired)
Pudelpointer
Retriever (Chesapeake Bay)
Retriever (Curly-coated)
Retriever (Flat-coated)
Retriever (Golden)

Retriever (Labrador)
Retriever (Nova Scotia Duck Tolling)
Setter (English)
Setter (Gordon)
Setter (Irish)
Spaniel (American Cocker)
Spaniel (American Water)
Spaniel (Blue Picardy)
Spaniel (Brittany)
Spaniel (Clumber)
Spaniel (English Cocker)
Spaniel (English Springer)
Spaniel (French)
Spaniel (Irish Water)
Spaniel (Sussex)
Spaniel (Welsh Springer)
Vizsla (Smooth-haired)
Weimaraner

Group 2 — Hounds
Bred to hunt game by sight or smell
Afghan Hound
Basenji
Bassett Hound
Beagle
Bloodhound
Borzoi
Coonhound (Black and Tan)
Dachshund (Miniature Long-haired)
Dachshund (Miniature Smooth)
Dachshund (Miniature Wire-haired)
Dachshund (Standard Long-haired)
Dachshund (Standard Smooth)
Dachshund (Standard Wire-haired)
Deerhound (Scottish)
Drever
Finnish Spitz
Greyhound
Harrier
Ibizan Hound
Irish Wolfhound
Norrbottenspets
Norwegian Elkhound

Kelley Good at K-9 Connections in Chilliwack (604-858-0196) is in the matchmaking business. Whatever you are looking for, she will find. She knows her breeds, and counsels families on good matches. Kelley is a certified trainer, breeder and groomer and has a veterinarian assistant certificate, so this was a natural extension of those skills. The charges are relatively low — never more than $25.

Norwegian Lundehund
Otterhound
Petit Basset Griffon Vendeen
Pharaoh Hound
Rhodesian Ridgeback
Saluki
Whippet

Group 3 — Working Dogs
Bred for guard and draft work
Akita
Alaskan Malamute
Bernese Mountain Dog
Boxer
Bullmastiff
Canaan Dog
Canadian Eskimo Dog
Doberman Pinscher
Entlebucher Mountain Dog
Eurasier
Great Dane
Great Pyrenees
Greenland Dog
Karelian Bear Dog
Komondor
Kuvasz
Leonberger
Mastiff
Newfoundland
Portuguese Water Dog
Rottweiler
St. Bernard
Samoyed
Schnauzer (Giant)
Schnauzer (Standard)
Siberian Husky

Group 4 — Terriers
Bred to go to ground after vermin
Airedale Terrier
American Staffordshire Terrier
Australian Terrier
Bedlington Terrier

Q: What do dogs put on their hot dogs?

A: Catsup.

Border Terrier
Bull Terrier
Cairn Terrier
Dandie Dinmont Terrier
Fox Terrier (Smooth)
Fox Terrier (Wire)
Irish Terrier
Kerry Blue Terrier
Lakeland Terrier
Manchester Terrier
Norfolk Terrier
Norwich Terrier
Schnauzer (Miniature)
Scottish Terrier
Sealyham Terrier
Skye Terrier
Soft-coated Wheaten Terrier
Staffordshire Bull Terrier
Welsh Terrier
West Highland White Terrier

Group 5 — Toys
Bred to be pets and lap dogs
Affenpinscher
Cavalier King Charles Spaniel
Chihuahua (Long Coat)
Chihuahua (Short Coat)
Chinese Crested Dog
English Toy Spaniel
Griffon (Brussels)
Italian Greyhound
Japanese Spaniel
Maltese
Mexican Hairless
Miniature Pinscher
Papillon
Pekingese
Pomeranian
Poodle (Toy)
Pug
Silky Terrier
Toy Manchester Terrier
Yorkshire Terrier

"Therefore to this dog will I,
Tenderly not scornfully,
Render praise and favour."
— Elizabeth Barrett
Browning,
"To Flush, My Dog"

Renaissance Rescue
(467-6045) is a loosely
organized group of dog
lovers who match people
who want dogs with dogs
who want people. Not
necessarily breed-specific.
Home visits are mandatory
before placing a dog.

Group 6 – Non-sporting Dogs
A variety of breeds not easily categorized
Bichon Frise
Boston Terrier
Bulldog
Chinese Shar-Pei
Chow Chow
Dalmatian
French Bulldog
Japanese Spitz
Keeshond
Lhasa Apso
Lowchen
Poodle (Miniature)
Poodle (Standard)
Schipperke
Shiba Inu
Shih Tzu
Tibetan Spaniel
Tibetan Terrier

Group 7 – Herding Dogs
Bred to herd sheep, cattle and other livestock
Australian Cattle Dog
Australian Shepherd
Bearded Collie
Belgian Sheepdog
Bouvier des Flandres
Briard
Collie (Rough)
Collie (Smooth)
German Shepherd Dog
Norwegian Buhund
Old English Sheepdog
Puli
Shetland Sheepdog
Swedish Vallhund
Welsh Corgi (Cardigan)
Welsh Corgi (Pembroke)

Canadian Kennel Club Miscellaneous Class
American Eskimo (Miniature)
American Eskimo (Standard)

Anatolian Shepherd Dog
Australian Kelpie
Caucasian Ovcharka (listed as Caucasus Shepherd Dog)
Cesky Terrier (listed as Bohemian Terrier)
Coton de Tulear
Fila Brasileiro
German Jagdterrier
German Pinscher
Havanese (listed as Bichon Havanais)
Münsterländer (Small)
Neapolitan Mastiff
Sarplaninac (listed as Yugoslavian Shepherd Dog)
Setter (Irish Red and White)
Spanish Mastiff
Tibetan Mastiff
Tosa Inu

Breeds Not Recognized by the CKC

These breeds are not recognized because they are not common in North America, are evolving as a breed or have opted out of the CKC program.

Akbash Dog
American Bulldog
Beauceron
Border Collie
Cane Corso
Catahoula Leopard Dog
Dogue de Bordeaux
Jack Russell Terrier
Perro de Presa Canario
Polish Owczarek Nizinny
Toy Fox Terrier

Besides the common "pack of dogs" and "litter of pups," James Lipton (in *An Exaltation of Larks*) suggests these further collective nouns: A kennel of dogs; a sleuth of hounds; a leash of Greyhounds; a cowardness of curs; a pomp of Pekingese; a waddle of Bassett Hounds; a vise of Pit Bulls; a howl of hounds and a piddle of puppies.

— James Lipton,
An Exaltation of Larks

MIXED BREED & UNREGISTERED DOGS

Tips on Finding a "Bitsy" Dog

The Dollar Dog

A dollar dog is all mixed
  up.
A bit of this, a bit of that.
We got ours when he was
  a pup
So small he slept in an old
  hat.
So small we borrowed a
  doll's beads
To make him his first collar.
Too small to see how many
  breeds
We got for just one dollar.
But not at all too small to
  see
He had an appetite.
An appetite? It seems to
  me
He ate up everything in
  sight!
The more he ate, the more
  we saw.
He got to be as big as two.
The more we saw, the
  more we knew
We had a genuine drooly-
  jaw,
Mishmash mongrel, all-
  around,
Flop-eared, bull-faced,
  bumble-paw,
Stub-tailed, short-haired,
  Biscuit Hound.
— John Ciardi

A "bitsy" dog is one that contains "bits of this, bits of that" — in other words, a dog that is not purebred. If you are looking for a dog without registration papers or for a mixed-breed dog, there are lots of ways to find it. The SPCA and the local pound are a good start. When you adopt a pet from a shelter, you may be preventing an unnecessary death. Most shelters allow you to take the dog for a walk before you adopt, which is a good practice.

Newspaper ads from individuals with dogs to sell or give away have some advantages too — you can usually see the puppy's mom, so you will get an idea of what your dog may look like. You will also be able to assess the situation in which it grew up. Never deal with anyone who doesn't give you straight answers, and if things feel wrong, leave.

Never give away a dog as a surprise gift. The recipient should participate in the selection. Instead of surprising the recipient, give a gift certificate for a fifteen-minute visit to a vet, or a photo of a dog with an IOU stating: "One dog to be selected later." Or call your local SPCA and ask how much a dog would cost there — and give that amount as a gift.

Adopting from Animal Shelters

Adoption Fees will vary between SPCA shelters and other organizations. To give you an idea of what it might cost, these are the adoption fees at the nine shelters of the SPCA Vancouver Regional Branch:

Already spayed/neutered — $65.00
Needs to be spayed/neutered — $115.00
Puppies — $125.00

Fees include an ID tattoo when the dog is spayed or neutered at the SPCA hospital, a spay/neuter certificate (value $50.00), and an examination to be performed within three business days of adoption, compliments of participating veterinarians.

Following is a list of animal shelters in the lower mainland:

Abbotsford SPCA
34312 Industrial Way
856-4600

Burnaby SPCA
3202 Norland
291-7201

Coquitlam SPCA
1414 Pipeline
942-4510

Delta SPCA
7450 80th St.
Ladner
946-7848

Langley Animal Control
26603 13th Ave.
856-7505

Maple Ridge SPCA
10235 Industrial
463-9511

Mission Pound
9541 Woodward St.
826-4496

New Westminster Pound
231 Ewen Ave.
526-5432

North Vancouver SPCA
299 Mansfield Place
988-7484

Richmond SPCA
12071 No. 5 Rd.
277-6212

Surrey SPCA
6706 152 St.
597-5655

Vancouver Pound
1280 Raymur Ave.
251-1325

Vancouver SPCA
1205 East 7th St.
879-7721

West Vancouver SPCA
1020 Marine Dr.
922-4622

White Rock Pound
South Surrry Veterinary
    Hospital
32nd Ave. and 140th St.
Surrey
Licenses: 541-2139
Animal Control: 541-2148

The Bank of Montreal has a British Columbia SPCA Vancouver Regional Branch MasterCard. Phone 879-1725 for information.

IMPORTANT DOG WELFARE ORGANIZATIONS

Listed below are some of the important organizations that will be referred to throughout this book. They can be of use right from the start — even as you consider whether or not to adopt a dog, and which dog might be right for you.

FIDO

The Western Federation of Individuals and Dog Organizations (FIDO) was formed in 1973 as an umbrella organization that would allow the dozens of dog clubs to work together. The idea was to give something back to the community, and to educate the public on being responsible pet owners. Here is FIDO's own description of their organization.

What is FIDO ?
— *FIDO*

FIDO was founded in 1973, incorporated under the Societies Act of British Columbia and is a registered charitable society. The objectives of FIDO are:

a) to provide liaisons and to promote communication among organizations, dog owners, government and the general public for the improvement of dog welfare;

b) to promote and provide education and services in matters affecting the welfare of dogs and other animals;

c) to work in conjunction with legislative bodies on matters relating to the sale, care, custody and control of dogs and other animals;

d) to provide information and services relating to the benefits of the human-animal bond.

FIDO maintains a telephone information service (681-1929) which the public can call to obtain information about dogs, including where to find specific breeds, training for dogs, and how to find help with any problem relating to dogs. The calls are returned by one of several

FIDO volunteers. There are 14 regular volunteers who work two shifts a day, and they return approximately 500 to 600 calls a month.

FIDO maintains a Tattoo Tracing Service through which lost dogs can be traced and returned to their rightful owners. Calls for assistance in tracing dogs are received from people throughout the province as well as others areas of Canada and the western United States. Thousands of dogs (plus cats and rabbits) have been traced since this service was established by FIDO in 1974.

FIDO provides public education, including *All About Pets*, a television show that can be seen on Community Cable, dog breeder seminars and clinics. It also provides a large selection of educational and informative material for distribution to the general public.

FIDO provides a mobile Information Booth at most dog shows in the Lower Mainland area. The booth also travels to shopping malls and special events. As a major component of FIDO's public education program, this booth provides information on many aspects of dog ownership, as well as activities relating to dogs.

FIDO organizes a visitation program to nursing homes, extended care hospitals, children's hospitals and rehabilitation centres as part of their Animal Assisted Activities and Therapy Programs.

FIDO was the major facilitator in the development of the Pacific Assistance Dogs Society (PADS, an affiliate of Canine Companions for Independence), a British Columbia program established to train dogs for people who have disabilities.

FIDO maintains liaisons with municipal and provincial governments, and offers assistance on matters relating to dogs and other animals and to monitor legislation relating to dogs. In response to requests from community representatives, FIDO has developed an Emergency Planning and Emergency Preparedness Program for the benefit of owners of animals throughout the province.

FIDO maintains a close working liaison with the BC Veterinary Medical Association and the SPCA on matters of mutual concern. FIDO is a member of Sport BC and the BC Recreation and Parks Association, and has worked closely with the Greater Vancouver Regional District (GVRD).

FIDO's Telephone Information Service keeps a list of breeders. Call: 681-1929

FIDO is a volunteer organization. All of the programs and services are the result of the work of many dedicated volunteers. In Vancouver, call: 681-1929

The SPCA

The British Columbia chapter of the Society to Prevent Cruelty to Animals opened in Victoria in 1895 and was modelled after the SPCA that opened in England in the 1840s. The SPCA exists to promote the human-animal bond and to educate people about the benefits of owning a pet and being responsible pet owners. The SPCA investigates reports of cruelty and neglect, as well as problems with large animals. It rescues animals trapped or in distress, and takes in strays. If the owners can't be found, the animals are adopted out. The SPCA is involved with disaster planning; the British Columbia SPCA (working alongside various government organizations and wildlife rescue agencies) is the main non-governmental organization responsible for rehabilitation of oiled birds.

The BC SPCA is an umbrella organization with 33 branches. One of those 33 is the Vancouver Regional Branch, which, in turn, has nine shelters. These are located in Abbotsford, Burnaby, Coquitlam, Delta, Maple Ridge, North Vancouver, Richmond, Surrey and Vancouver. The West Vancouver SPCA is a separate branch. For addresses and phone numbers, see "Adopting from Animal Shelters" (page 38).

Other Small Animal Welfare Organizations

Citizens Pet Population Control Society
Vancouver
325-1579
Provides financial assistance for spaying/neutering and shots for pets belonging to low income people. Holds bazaars and raffles to raise funds.

Delta Society
289 Perimeter Road East
Renton, WA
98055-1329

The Original Story of the Human/Animal Bond

Old Mother Hubbard went to the cupboard to get her poor dog a bone
But when she came there, the cupboard was bare, and so the poor Dog had none.
She went to the baker's to buy him some bread,
But when she came back the poor Dog was dead.
She went to the joiner's to buy him a coffin,
But when she came back the poor dog was laughing.
She took a clean dish to get him some tripe,
But when she came back, he was smoking a pipe.
She went to the ale house to get him some beer,
But when she came back, the Dog sat in a chair.
She went to the tavern for white wine and red,
But when she came back, the Dog stood on his head.
She went to the barber's to buy him a wig.
But when she came back he was dancing a jig.
She went to the hatter's to buy him a hat,

(800) 869-6898 (voice); (800) 809-2714 (TDD)
website: http://petsforum.com/deltasociety/
A United States-based organization, Delta Society
distributes human-animal bond and pet therapy
information.

Doris Orr Needy Animals Trust Endowment (DONATE)

North Vancouver
987-9015
DONATE provides advice for people trying to find
homes for their animals. Orr suggests ways to keep the
animals; if that is impossible, she will help find homes
for them. She will also match an animal to a person
looking to adopt a pet. Doris Orr has been in business
for 30 years. She does not shelter animals.

The Human-Animal Bond Association of Canada

P.O. Box 71012, Maplehurst Postal Outlet
Burlington, Ontario
L7T 4J8
e-mail: habac@glen-net.ca
The human-animal bond is the relationship between pets
and people. The Human-Animal Bond Association of
Canada is an organization dedicated to educating the
medical community and politicians about the positive
effects of animal companionship.

Humane Education Animal League (HEAL)

Langley
856-5749
Founder Cornelia Heal brings 20 years of training
experience to this volunteer-run organization. HEAL is
a foster-care shelter for dogs and cats, and focusses on
breed counselling for people who want to adopt a pet
from them. They ask for a $100 fee for each animal,
which covers the cost of spaying/neutering, all shots
and a tattoo. If the adoption doesn't work out, HEAL
will take the animal back. HEAL also provides free petsitting for a number of women's shelters in the Lower
Mainland and emergency sitting services for people who
may have been forced out of their home by fire.

But when she came back
  he was feeding the cat.
She went to the fruiter's to
  buy him some fruit,
But when she came back
  he was playing the flute.
She went to the tailor's to
  buy him a coat,
But when she came back
  he was riding a goat.
She went to the cobbler's
  to buy him some shoes,
But when she came back
  he was reading the news.
She went to the seamstress
  to buy him some linen,
But when she came back
  the Dog was a-spinning.
She went to the hosier's to
  buy him some hose,
But when she came back
  we was dressed in his
  clothes.
The Dame made a curtsy,
  the Dog made a bow,
The Dame said, "your
  servant", the Dog said,
  "Bow wow"
This wonderful dog was
  Dame Hubbard's delight,
He could sing, he could
  dance, he could read, he
  could write.
She gave him rich dainties
  whenever he fed.
And erected a monument
  when he was dead.

Mercy Volunteers for Animals Society
Vancouver
254-7047
Mercy provide information on dogs available for adoption in the pound. They also provide financial assistance to low income families who wish to own a dog or need a dog spayed. Mercy has a wide variety of literature on dogs and are active in dog advocacy.

The University of British Columbia Chair in Animal Welfare
Suite 248 - 2357 Main Mall
Vancouver
V6T 1Z4
822-2493
UBC is trying to set up a Chair in Animal Welfare position and needs donations to help do so. The chair will be held by a scientist and educator who will concentrate on teaching, research and public education on animal welfare issues.

Vancouver Dog Owners Association
Glen Swain
736-4640
Formed in 1997 in reaction to the increased enforcement of fines against dogs off-leash. This is a a group of responsible dog owners who care about the physical and emotional well-being of their pets, and believe that the exercise a dog gets running and playing off-leash is far superior to what it can get on-leash. They are looking for supporters as they work with the Park Board and the Animal Control Officers to find a compromise in the city of Vancouver.

Vancouver Humane Society
P.O. Box 18119
2225 W. 41st Ave.
Vancouver
266-9744
A grassroots community organization dedicated to exposing animal abuse in the community and working towards practical and positive change. They have a bi-annual newsletter called *Animal Alert*.

West Coast Spay and Neuter Society (SANS)
Mary Evans
Mission
228-1126
SANS shelters abandoned dogs and cats and provides access to low-cost spay and neuter facilities. Sheltered animals are spayed/neutered and fed until they find homes. The shelter has about 40 dogs at any one time, and most dogs are sheltered in Mission. SANS is a registered charity and charges $100 for adoption to cover spay/neuter, shots, de-worming and tattooing.

Wywanda Humane Education Resource Centre
Evelyn Oberg
Vancouver
534-4673
An extensive research library of resources run by a retired breeder with a special interest in genetics, nutrition and prevention of problems with dogs. Available for small group workshops by appointment.

"I like a bit of mongrel myself, whether it's a man or a dog; they're the best for everyday."
— George Bernard Shaw

FIRE HOSE

Portrait by
Julia Morton

II. Good Dog Owner Etiquette

Can you honestly call yourself an RDO? That's a Responsible Dog Owner, and hopefully this book is preaching to the converted — but we can all see our less-than-perfect selves in these pages somewhere. Sit, stay, come and down: Does your dog do it every time, everywhere? Just as few of us think of ourselves as bad drivers, rarely will anyone admit to being a bad dog owner. But we all know them. We know owners whose attitude towards dog doo is to kick rather than pick. We know dogs that are perfectly obedient until a squirrel darts past. And we know of horror stories where an off-leash dog has mauled a five-year-old, even though the owner insists that his dog loves children.

This chapter reminds us of our legal responsibilities to our dog and to the public. As well, it addresses how we can co-exist with other creatures such as coyotes, what to do when a dog is lost, the hard facts on leashing and tethering, spaying and neutering, and what to do with doo. Much of this chapter is common sense. Still, as responsible dog owners we have a duty to pass on information so that we can all act responsibly and live together harmoniously.

ARE YOU A RESPONSIBLE DOG OWNER?

Test Your Dog Owner Etiquette

— *FIDO*

Here's a quick way to test your dog-owner etiquette. Consider yourself a Responsible Dog Owner if you can answer "yes" to the following questions.

- Are you aware that our community has a serious problem with too many unwanted, uncontrolled, stray and abandoned dogs?
- A large number of the dogs and puppies taken to animal shelters have to be destroyed because there are no homes for them. Do you agree that it would be better if they had not been born in the first place?
- Do you know that it is *not* necessary for the health or personality of a female dog to have one litter before it is spayed?
- Do you know that letting a dog have one litter so that children can see the miracle of birth is contributing to the overpopulation of dogs?
- Is your dog spayed or neutered?
- Do you realize that it is an act of cruelty to abandon an animal?
- Are you financially able and morally committed to caring for your dog for its natural life of perhaps 10 to 15 years?
- Do you keep your dog from running loose in your neighbourhood and trespassing on your neighbour's property?
- Do you control your dog's barking?
- Is your dog licensed?
- Does your dog have proper inoculations against infectious diseases?
- Are you knowledgeable about animal control laws in your community and willing to obey them?
- Do you set a good example to children by really caring for your dog and demonstrating kindness toward it?

TAKING LEGAL RESPONSIBILITY FOR YOUR DOG

Dogs and the Law

— British Columbia Dial-a-Law,
Canadian Bar Association

The following information on dogs and the law in British Columbia is for general use only. It is not legal advice. If you do have a specific legal question or problem, you should talk to a lawyer.

In general, each municipality can make its own rules on dog ownership. If you have a complaint, check with your own municipality to see if they have passed a by-law on the issue. If you own a dog, you should be familiar with the legal responsibilities that go with ownership. To find out exactly what those responsibilities are, you must look at local by-laws, provincial statutes, the Criminal Code and the common law.

Local By-laws

Each municipality has its own set of by-laws, and this is where you will find all the licensing provisions and rules about where dogs are and aren't allowed. You can find a copy of your local by-laws at your public library or courthouse library or at your municipal hall. Many municipalities have passed by-laws to prohibit dogs from running at large. In Vancouver, for example, owners must keep their dogs under immediate charge or control when away from their own home. Dogs are not allowed on the street or in a public place unless they're on a leash that is not more than eight feet long, and they are never allowed on bathing beaches.

Photograph by
Kent Southwell

The Vancouver Pound by-law also includes provisions regulating "vicious" dogs, which are defined to include pit bulls and similar breeds plus dogs with a known propensity to attack or bite without provocation. The by-law requires these dogs to be muzzled or kept securely indoors or in a pen. A dog that has bitten a person may be seized and impounded for up to three weeks.

If any dog is found running at large or unlicensed, it will be taken to the pound and kept there for three days. Then, unless it's claimed in the meantime, it will be put up for sale — if it seems likely that it could be sold — or destroyed. The owner could also be charged with a violation of the pertinent by-law, and may end up in criminal court, liable to a fine. If the dog is sick or injured when it's picked up, it may be destroyed immediately or sent to the SPCA.

Health by-laws in Vancouver and elsewhere make it illegal to bring any dog, except a "seeing-eye dog," into any establishment where food is kept or handled in any way, unless the establishment is a private home. Vancouver also has a "pooper scooper" by-law which stipulates that if your dog leaves excrement on property that's not your own, it's up to you to remove it or face a fine of anywhere from $50 to $500. (This doesn't apply to seeing-eye dogs, of course.)

The noise by-laws apply to dogs, too. If you live in Vancouver, for example, and your neighbors complain that your dog's barking disturbs the peace and quiet of the neighborhood, you could be liable to a fine of $50 to $2,000, or even up to two months in jail.

The Provincial Statute

If you don't live in a municipality, then you will have to look at the provincial Livestock Protection Act for information on your legal responsibilities. Here again, the statute stipulates that dogs must be licensed and those running at large will be impounded. There are also a number of provisions aimed at protecting farm animals from attacks by dogs. For instance, dogs running in a pack — and that means any two or more dogs — can be killed by a police officer or any other authorized person. And anyone can kill a dog on the spot if it's seen running at large and attacking or viciously chasing a person or

Seen on Pavlov's door:
"Knock. Don't ring bell."

domestic animal. In some cases, the owner of an animal that has been killed or injured by a dog can claim compensation from the provincial government for the financial loss. The dog owner can be made to pay back to the government up to one half of the compensation paid out. The Livestock Protection Act also gives Provincial Court judges the authority to order a dog be destroyed if it has killed or injured a person or domestic animal, or is likely to do so.

The Criminal Code

The Criminal Code deals with each owner's responsibility to his or her dog, and also the owner's responsibility to others who may be injured by the dog. First of all, it's a crime in Canada if you willfully cause unnecessary pain, suffering or injury to any animal. If it can be shown that you failed to take reasonable care of your dog, you could face a fine or jail term and a criminal record. Second, if you don't take reasonable care to avoid endangering the safety of others, and your dog attacks and injures someone, you could be charged with the offense of criminal negligence.

Q: What do you get when you cross Lassie with a cantelope?

A: A melon-collie baby.

Common Law

Quite apart from your criminal liability, if your dog injures someone, the victim may sue you in the civil courts. If they're successful, you will have to pay compensation for the injuries. You should check with your insurance agent to find out whether you would be covered by your household insurance policy if that should ever happen. Better yet, if you have a dog that is likely to bite or attack a person, keep it under control at all times or get rid of it. Even if your dog has never bitten anyone, you could be liable for that first bite if it can be shown that the dog has a fierce or vicious nature. If the dog is vicious by nature, you keep it at your own risk whether or not it has actually bitten or injured anyone. You may be liable even if the dog injures someone while on your own property or tied up. If your dog has actually bitten someone before and does so again, you will be held liable no matter how careful you are to keep it under control.

Clearly, there are a lot of responsibilities involved in owning a dog. If you live in a municipality, you must have a license for the dog and keep the animal on your property or on a leash. If you're outside a municipality, you also must take care that your dog doesn't endanger livestock or start running with other dogs. Wherever you live, you have a legal responsibility to take care of your dog and to ensure that it doesn't injure anyone.

To reach Dial-a-Law, call 687-4680, or, outside the Greater Vancouver toll-free area, 1-800-565-LAWS (5297). To reach the Dial-a-Law website, go to: http://www.acjnet.org/dialalaw/bc.html

Animal Control By-laws in Vancouver

— The City of Vancouver Dog Hotline (871-MUTT)

The Park Board is getting tougher on owners who let their dogs run off leash in Vancouver's parks. In the spring of 1997 they hired a special beach-patrol officer whose sole purpose is to ticket owners of off-leash dogs. In the previous year, the Park Board had received 11,000

Photograph by
Ellice Hauta

incident complaints (for biting and off-leash dogs, among other things) – and they aren't the only ones who get complaints. The Vancouver Pound heard 3,039 dog complaints in 1996; of those, 335 were complaints about vicious dogs. In Vancouver, it's the pound's job to enforce dog licensing, deal with dog complaints and remove dead dogs and cats from the streets. (Pounds perform similar tasks in Langley, Mission, New Westminster and White Rock. In Abbotsford, Burnaby, Coquitlam, Delta, Maple Ridge, North Vancouver, Richmond, Surrey and West Vancouver, these jobs fall to the SPCA).

So far, the Vancouver Pound's success rate in enforcing licensing is not great. They estimate that there are 60,000 dogs in Vancouver and that only 15,800 or so are licensed. In 1996, 6,541 dogs ended up at the pound. Of those, 2,644 were adopted, 782 were returned to the owner, 1,900 were euthanized at the owner's request, 502 were euthanized because they weren't adopted, 243 were killed on the street and were dead on arrival, 445 were transferred out to foster homes or shelters, and seven are listed as "other". The pound makes its money through licensing and impounding fees, but the $535,000 raised in 1996 didn't cover that year's operating cost of $699,000. Licenses aren't that expensive. For an un-neutered dog the cost is $54 and for a neutered dog it's $34. The license ensures your dog is always identifiable to neighbours and to animal control officers should they find your dog at large. Your dog will be returned to you quickly and safely if it is licensed.

There are three by-laws that deal with dogs and the ways in which you can avoid paying fines or having to retrieve your dog from the pound. The following rules are summarized from the Canine Waste By-law, the Animal Control By-law and the Parks Control By-law:

- Dogs over three months old must be licensed.
- Unlicensed dogs or dogs at large may be impounded.
- If a dog is seized because it has allegedly bitten someone, it can be held for up to 21 days.
- Dogs are not allowed on bathing beaches or in water near a bathing beach.
- Vicious dogs must be muzzled when not on the owner's property.
- Owners must scoop their dog's poop.

A dog walked into a bar with a cast on his leg and said: "I want the man who shot my paw!"

- Noise from barking dogs is not allowed if it can be heard off the owner's property.
- The maximum number of dogs allowed on a single premise is three.

Here are the specifics of some pertinent by-laws for Vancouver. (Owners in each of the nearby municipalities should check for similar by-laws in their area.)

Animal Control By-law #7528 Sec. 4.1

No person owning, possessing or harbouring any dog shall permit, suffer or allow the same to run at large within the City.

Animal Control By-law #7528 Sec. 4.2: Leashing

Dogs are not allowed to run at large in the City of Vancouver. Dogs must be on a leash and under full custody and control of a competent person when off the owner's property.

Animal Control By-law #7528 Sec. 5.1: Licenses

Every person who is the owner, possessor or harbourer of a dog over the age of three months is required to obtain an annual license for his/her dog. These licenses are due and payable January 1.

Animal Control By-law #7528 Sec. 2(10): Vicious Dogs

"Vicious Dog" means:

- any dog with a known propensity, tendency or disposition to attack or provoke any domestic animals or humans; or
- any dog which has bitten another domestic animal or human without provocation; or
- a Pit Bull Terrier, American Pit Bull Terrier, Pit Bull, Staffordshire Bull Terrier, American Staffordshire Terrier or any dog of mixed breeding which includes any of the aforementioned breeds.

Animal Control By-law #7528 Sec. 4.4: Muzzling

In addition to being on a leash when off the owner's property, a vicious dog must be muzzled to prevent it from biting another animal or person.

Anti-cruelty Laws:
The Province of BC has a Prevention of Cruelty to Animals Act. Under the Police Act, SPCA field officers are special provincial constables. Only the SPCA has the authority to enforce the PCA Act. The SPCA is the body that investigates, seizes or destroys any animals suffering from cruelty or neglect; it is also authorized to charge people causing distress to an animal.

Animal Control By-law #7528 Sec. 4.5: Confinement

Every owner possessor or harbourer of a vicious dog shall at all times, while the dog is on the premises owned or controlled by such person, keep the dog securely confined either indoors or in an enclosed pen or other structure capable of preventing the entry of young children and adequately constructed to prevent the dog from escaping.

Animal Control By-law #7528 Sec. 4.9: Impounding

If a dog is off the owner's property and not on a leash nor under the immediate charge of a responsible person it will be impounded or the owner will be summonsed for breach of the Animal Control By-law.

> My neighbour's dog is a snob. His name is Fido, but he spells it Phydeaux.

Animal Control By-law #7528 Sec. 4.3: Beaches

It is unlawful to bring a dog to any bathing beach whether it is on a leash or not.

Animal Control By-law #7528 Sec. 4.13: Biting Dog

A dog which has bitten a person may be seized and impounded for a period of up to 21 days.

Animal Control By-law #7528 Sec. 6.1: Dog Waste

The owner, or any person having the care, custody or control of a dog, shall remove forthwith any excrement deposited by said dog. (This does not apply to dog owner's property.)

Special Noise By-law #6555 Sec. 4(C): Dog Barking

No person shall allow their dog to bark in such a manner that the barking can easily be heard by an individual or member of the public who is not on the same premises as the barking dog.

For more information on dog rules in the city of Vancouver, call: 871-MUTT (the City of Vancouver Dog Hotline).

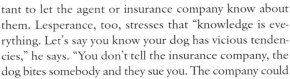
LIABILITY INSURANCE FOR DOG OWNERS

— Mike Grenby

Don't let your dog bite your wallet — and, while you're at it, keep an eye on any boarders you may have, or the customers in your home-based business. While we Canadians aren't as prone to launching large lawsuits as our American cousins, it is still a good idea for those of us who are dog owners to make sure our liability coverage is in order.

A homeowner's policy typically includes basic liability insurance, usually for a minimum $500,000 and sometimes for as much as $1 million. "But tenants in particular are vulnerable," says lawyer Bob Lesperance, of Lesperance Mendes Mancuso. "They often don't have liability coverage because they feel their possessions don't warrant taking out a tenant's policy." Adds Dick White, of Oakridge Insurance Agencies Limited: "Homeowners might not think to notify their agent or insurance company if there is a material change in the use of their property. Perhaps you start up a home business, with customers or clients coming and going. Or you take in boarders, either on a regular basis or the occasional student now and then during the year." When these changes occur in the use of your property, it is important to let the agent or insurance company know about them. Lesperance, too, stresses that "knowledge is everything. Let's say you know your dog has vicious tendencies," he says. "You don't tell the insurance company, the dog bites somebody and they sue you. The company could

Relief sculpture by
Steve Hall

refuse to pay the claim. Or what happens if you are looking after somebody else's dog and there's a lawsuit. Would you be covered?"

Lesperance also cites the case of an injured motorcyclist who recently won a damage award of $233,000 (reduced on appeal to $114,000) because a 10-month-old Labrador retriever escaped from its pen and ran onto an adjoining road where it collided with the motorcycle. The collision injured the rider and killed the dog. The judge said the dog's owners had a duty to control the dog so it couldn't escape and cause injury to people using the road. "Damages could reach into the millions of dollars if the injuries are catastrophic, which could easily have been the case with the motorcyclist," Lesperance says. It's particularly important for both dog owners and parents to take reasonable care when allowing small children to come into contact with dogs. "The dog might have no vicious tendencies and no history of snapping at children," says Lesperance. "Still, the dog might bite a child who pulls its tail. So the owner might be liable through negligence if he or she doesn't warn the child or an adult against pulling its tail."

For homeowners, a single umbrella liability policy is usually the least expensive way to increase coverage on several assets like principal residence, vacation home, boat, plane and (in most provinces/territories) cars. If you aren't sure about your liability coverage, talk to a general insurance agent now. Often, raising the limit to $1 million from $500,000 could cost as little as $10. It's a worthwhile investment for every responsible dog- and property-owner.

Q: What do you get when you cross an agnostic with a dyslexic insomniac?

A: Someone who lies awake at night pondering the existence of doG.

LEASHING & TETHERING

Leash It or Lose It

— Greater Vancouver Regional District (GVRD)

Here are some facts you may not have known about the benefits of keeping your dog leashed:

- Unleashed dogs, especially small ones, can be prey for coyotes and eagles.
- Unleashed dogs can pick up diseases through contact with other animals and birds or their feces.
- You may know that you can control your dog if it's off leash. But can you control another dog that approaches, running free and behaving aggressively?
- Leashing is the best way to prevent an injury to your dog resulting from fights with other dogs.
- If your dog harms someone you may be personally liable.

This is a Leash

— FIDO

Here are more of the advantages of a leash:

- It is the best birth control device, preventing random matings and unwanted puppies.
- It is the best way to keep your dog uninjured, restrain your dog from darting into traffic and eliminate pain and veterinary bills.
- It is the best good-neighbour policymaker, keeping your dog from any sort of trespassing, destructive or otherwise, on your neighbor's lands or on the city's sidewalks. It will also keep your dog from jumping up on people and possibly inflicting an injury, or causing discomfort or fright.
- It is the best identification service, as the license tag attached to the collar will get your dog back to you if the dog should become lost.
- It is the best wildlife service, keeping your dog from harassing deer and other wild animals, either by itself or as part of a wild dog pack.
- It is the bet way to develop an affectionate dog. The

touch of the leash gives your dog definite assurance that it is protected, loved and wanted.

- It is the best crime prevention device: When the leash is not in use, your dog will be at home, overseeing matters and protecting its "family."

Keep your dog leashed as a habit and as a matter of civil practice.

Tethering Dogs

Richmond, Surrey, Burnaby, and North and West Vancouver have by-laws that require dog owners to give their dogs regular un-fettered exercise. Vancouver does not have any such by-law, so there is no policy on tethering up dogs. This needs to change. Below are the recommendations of the SPCA on this issue.

Against Tethering
— British Columbia SPCA

You see one in every community: a dog tied day after day to a back porch or fence, lying lonely on a pad of bare, packed dirt. The water bowl, if there is one, is usually empty or just out of reach. Abandoned but chained-up backyard dogs cannot move to find comfort, shelter or companionship. In winter, they shiver; in summer, they languish. Year-round, they suffer.

Of course, dogs can be forced to live outside, alone and away from their human pack, but to force this kind of life on a dog is one of the worst things you can do. Being alone goes against the dog's most basic instinct. If you doubt this, think of all the whining, barking, clawing dogs you have seen tied alone outside. These dogs are trying desperately to get the attention of their human families.

People who keep their dogs constantly tied outside rationalize their actions, saying that they do spend time with the dogs. But even the most well-meaning among them do not spend significant time with their animal companions. Under the best of circumstances, the backyard dog gets a bowl of food and water, a quick pat on the head and maybe a few minutes of contact with another living being each day.

> "And in that town a dog was found,
> As many dogs there be,
> Both mongrel, puppy, whelp, and hound,
> And curs of low degree."
> — Oliver Goldsmith,
> "An Elegy on the Death of a Mad Dog"

Dogs can offer people the gifts of steadfast devotion, abiding love and joyful companionship. Unless a person is willing to accept these offerings and take the time to return them in kind, it would be best for him or her not to get a dog. A sad, lonely, bewildered dog tied out back only suffers — and what sort of person wants to maintain suffering?

A Policy on the Tethering of Dogs

The British Columbia SPCA strongly opposes the indiscriminate chaining or tethering of dogs without due regard for their physical and/or psychological well-being. The society insists that, if a dog is to be tethered, the methods and equipment used must be humane and not likely to cause any physical or mental harm. The British Columbia SPCA offers these minimum standards/guidelines:

1. Chain shall be a minimum of two metres in length.
2. Weight of chain shall not exceed 30 grams per metre.
3. Links of chain shall not exceed an opening of 20 millimetres.
4. Collars shall be nylon or leather and must be properly fitted. Puppies must be checked regularly to ensure the collar is not too tight.
5. Choke-type collars shall not be used.
6. Inverted studded-type collars shall not be used.
7. A swivel hook shall be used to fasten chain at either end.
8. Running line shall be a minimum of 10 metres long.
9. Running line shall be metal, and not less than 10 millimetres in thickness.
10. Running line shall be no higher than half a metre above ground where low system is used and shall be not less than 2 metres from ground where a high system is used.
11. Running line shall be free of obstacles, allowing for unobstructed operation, and be removed from embankments, roof tops etc., in order to avoid accidental hanging of dog.
12. Spill-proof container shall be provided with clean, potable drinking water in sufficient quantity to satisfy the dog's needs.

"Don't look now, dear, I'll tell you about it afterwards."
— Winston Churchill, to his poodle Rufus, covering his eyes while they watch the scene in *Oliver Twist* where Bill Sikes is about to kill his dog.

13. Dog shall have access to shelter to ensure protection from heat, cold, wet and drafts.
14. Dog shall receive exercise, human companionship and socialization for at least two hours in every 24.
15. Dog shall be given proper food to maintain normal good health.
16. Dog shall be provided with necessary medical care.
17. Food and water receptacles, as well as general area where animal is kept, shall be sanitized and cleaned on a regular basis.
18. Appropriate signs shall be placed in conspicuous places to caution people regarding the presence of a dog.

A man running a little behind schedule arrives at a picture theatre, goes in to watch the movie that has already started, and as his eyes adjust to the darkness, he is surprised to see a dog sitting beside its master in the row ahead, intently watching the movie. It even seems to be enjoying the movie: wagging its tail in the happy bits, drooping its ears at the sad bits, and hiding its eyes with its paws at the scary bits.

After the movie, the man approaches the dog's owner and says, "Jeez mate, your dog really seemed to enjoy the movie. I'm amazed!"

"Yes, I'm amazed also," came the reply. "He hated the book."

Photograph by
Lionel Trudel

61

SPAY/NEUTERING INFORMATION

The Facts of Life

— The British Columbia SPCA

Here are the facts of life about spaying and neutering your dog.

The Problem
In seven years, one dog and her offspring can produce over 4,000 dogs (with an average litter size of four, once a year).

The Solution
- Have your own dog spayed or neutered.
- Encourage friends, family and neighbours to have their animals spayed and neutered.
- Sponsor the spaying and neutering of a shelter animal.
- Volunteer to do adoption follow-up at your local animal shelter to ensure that people who have adopted animals have complied with the spay/neuter requirement in their adoption agreement.

These are some common questions about spaying and neutering:

What do "spaying" and "neutering" mean?
Spaying and neutering are surgical procedures used to prevent dogs from reproducing. In a female animal, spaying consists of removing the uterus and ovaries. The technical term is ovario-hysterectomy. For a male animal, neutering involves the removal of the testicles; this is known as castration.

Do spaying and neutering hurt?
The surgery is done under a general anesthetic, which makes it painless. The operation for both males and females is straightforward and low risk. Recovery is usually uneventful. The worst your dog might experience is some discomfort for a short time after the operation.

When should spaying or neutering take place?

The usual recommendation is that the dog should have the operation when it is six to seven months old. Your veterinarian should be consulted to determine the best time for your dog.

Shouldn't a female dog have one litter first?

Allowing a female dog to produce a litter does not have any benefits. In fact, there are health risks for the mother during the pregnancy and when giving birth.

Will my dog become fat and lazy once it is sterilized?

No. Your dog will actually benefit from spaying or neutering because it will lead a healthier and longer life. Pets become fat and lazy as a result of overeating and a lack of exercise, not from spaying or neutering. Furthermore, spaying a female eliminates the possibility of her developing uterine and/or ovarian cancer and greatly reduces the chance of breast cancer. Neutering a male reduces the incidence of prostate enlargement and prostate cancer.

Will sterilization change my dog's personality?

Generally not. For a female there is virtually no change at all. For males sterilization usually results in a diminishing of some aggressive behaviours. Spayed/neutered dogs are free from sexual anxiety and are, therefore, calmer and more content to stay at home. Also, if you have more than one dog, you will find they get along much better if they are all spayed or neutered.

What is it going to cost to spay or neuter my dog?

The cost of spaying or neutering your dog depends on many factors. For example, a large dog will cost more than a small dog; if your dog is overweight or in season this can also add to the cost. Contact your veterinarian to get a more accurate idea of the costs involved for your dog. The cost of spaying or neutering is really quite small when compared to what you will spend on food for your dog over its lifetime. Also consider the possible costs if you do not spay and neuter. If your dog should wander off in search of a mate, you may be faced with paying

Sirius is another name for the Dog Star, the most dominant star in the constellation *Canis Major* (Larger Dog). The word Sirius comes from the Greek word *seirius*, meaning scorching. In ancient Greece, Sirius' rising at dawn just before sunrise marked the start of the hottest part of the summer, hence the expression "the dog days of summer."

fines and impoundment costs. You may also be faced with the additional costs of maintaining puppies or kittens. Worse yet, think of the costs should your dog be injured while roaming for a mate. Having your dog spayed or neutered is part of being a responsible dog owner.

The official goal of the British Columbia SPCA is to reach zero euthanasia of adoptable animals — and we are making real progress. Through school programs and public education, as well as the mandatory spaying and neutering of animals adopted from our shelters and subsidized spaying and neutering for people experiencing financial hardship, our goal can be achieved.

WHAT TO DO WITH DOO?

Legally you can do only three things with dog waste:
- Bury it in your yard or use a doggie septic tank;
- flush it down your toilet;
- have a service pick it up and take it away.

Here's an article that appeared in the *Vancouver Sun*, addressing the problem of just what to do with doggy doo.

Dogged by Messy Garbage

— Doug Sagi

You may occasionally argue with a police officer, denounce the mail carrier as a fool or get into a fight with the income tax people, but it is a foolhardy individual who offends his garbage collector. Indeed, the collectors are best treated with courtesy. Call them what they ask to be called, be it "refuse disposal technician" or "sanitation engineer." It is thoughtful to leave them cool drinks on warm days and remember them at the holiday season.

Offend the garbage collectors and they have the ultimate recourse. They will refuse to serve. The remonstration is firm and absolute. If they do not like your garbage, they will refuse to collect it. They are within their rights, according to Vancouver's — and most other municipalities' — by-laws. What you put into your garbage may well be your business, but if the garbage collectors do not like it, it is not their business to pick it up and put it in their trucks.

There is a rule against putting "offensive" material in household garbage, and at the top of the list of things garbage persons do not want to collect is dog droppings. "Particularly when people save up a yard full of the stuff and put it in a plastic bag. It gets thrown into the truck and compressed and it bursts. If you are standing behind the truck, you get showered with it. That is offensive," explains Larry Balla of the Vancouver sanitation service.

People are not supposed to put dog doo in the garbage, but it is a rule often violated. Balla says dog

A dog walks into Western Union and asks the clerk to send a telegram. He fills out a form on which he writes down the telegram he wishes to send: "Bow wow wow, Bow wow wow."

The clerk says, "You can add another 'Bow wow' for the same price."

"I don't think so," the dog responds. "Wouldn't that sound a little silly?"

droppings should be flushed down toilets or buried in yards. This is what your garbage person will advise when you are caught with the droppings in your garbage can.

This can be inconvenient. Dog droppings do not flush easily, especially when the only time you get around to it is when you mow the lawn and there are four kilos of the little brown nuisances. There is a way, however, to dispose of dog doo with almost no trouble and no expense. Build your own dog doo disposal system, or DDDS. Intelligent dog owners have been using them for years. They are easy to make, convenient to use, as environmentally friendly as cloth diapers, and, believe it or not, odor-free. Like many home improvement projects, you can go expensive or inexpensive, custom-made or home-made. You can buy a DDDS from a department store, but there is no need. What you do need is a spade, a well-made plastic basin (or dish pan), an old garbage can top or piece of plywood for a lid and a package of septic tank starter. The starter costs $2 or $3 for a small box of four packets and is available in most supermarkets.

Find a spot in the back yard that is well-drained and somewhat out of the way, but handy enough to get to with a trowel full of the day's offerings. You do not want it under a tree because you do not want roots growing into it. Dig a hole about half a metre deep and 30 centimetres in diameter. Take some time to make a neat hole. It should be big enough to contain the plastic basin at the bottom.

Collect the dog doo and drop it into the basin. (If you haven't cleaned up for more than a week, be sensible and put no more than a couple of days supply in the basin.) Sprinkle two of the packets of septic tank starter on top of the dog doo and add a litre or so of water. Cover the hole with the lid.

Within 48 hours, the septic tank starter, which is non-caustic, promoting natural bacterial growth, will have begun its work and you can add more dog doo. Add the dog doo daily. Give the system a bucket of water once a week and a packet of starter (one of the four

Much asked question: What's with the macho factor? The bigger the guy, the bigger the dog, the rarer the picking up of poo. In fact, it is the observation of most women that it is usually guys who don't pick up dog doo.

Make our day: Prove us wrong!

in the box) once or twice a month. The dog doo turns to liquid, most of which washes away, dissolved by the bacteria. What remains is a humus that collects at such a slow rate it need only be dug out and spread around the yard every two or three years.

The DDS does not smell, even on the warmest summer days, though the basin may need an extra pail of water now and then. The system will not work in freezing temperatures, but it perks along through much of a Lower Mainland winter. (You can probably avoid offending your garbage collector by making well-wrapped packages during the cold months.) The Vancouver health department says the DDDS is okay as long as the neighbours do not complain — fortunately, the neighbours will have nothing to complain about.

Some of us are now working on training the dog to lift the lid to drop in the deposits directly...but there is some difficulty in getting male dogs to close the lid after they've finished!

Q: How can you tell a tree from a dog?

A: By its bark.

Dog Doo Services: Business is Picking Up

Each week, you can have someone else pick up your pail of doo, dispose of it and leave you a clean bucket to fill again. Many of these services take the excrement to the GVRD waste treatment plant on Iona Island; others have their own disposal set-ups with farmers or other interested people. Prices range from $4.50 to $7 a week to pick up a pail, to $10 for picking up the yard as well.

Delta Doggy Doo
Harley Rea
813-4515
Ladner, Tsawwassen, North Delta and Richmond.

Doggone Pet Waste Removal Service
Doug Atkinson
739-1234
West Side of Vancouver and some areas of East Vancouver.

The Pooper Scooper
Gary Godwin
258-0652
Abbotsford to Richmond, excluding Vancouver.

Scooby's Dog Waste Removal Service: The Originals (since 1992)
Craig Stark and Scott Davis
926-8180
Burnaby to Coquitlam, Richmond, the West Side and the North Shore.

Valley Pet Taxi & Services Ltd.
855-1419
Mission, Aldergrove, Abbotsford and parts of Langley.

URBAN COYOTES

The Urban Coyote Project

— Kristine Webber

Coyotes are an extremely adaptable wildlife species that survives well in urban environments. They are relatively new to the Lower Mainland, but have lived in large cities like Calgary and Los Angeles for many years. Coyotes are often sighted on local golf courses and in parks, and they can be found in most Vancouver neighbourhoods.

Coyotes look much like a cross between a small collie and a German Shepherd. Although there is variation in colour, coyotes generally have a grizzled reddish-brown coat interspersed with darker mane hairs and lighter undersides. Coyotes in the Lower Mainland weigh between 9 and 14 kilograms. They often appear heavier than they actually are due to their thick double coat, and may appear taller because of their long legs. They can use these long legs to run up to 64 kilometres per hour for short distances. While running, they hold their thick bushy tails low.

Coyotes eat a variety of food: In rural and wild environments, up to 70 percent of a coyote's diet consists of small mammals (mice, voles, rabbits etc.). The rest of their diet is a combination of fruits, vegetables, insects, garbage and other available items. In urban areas, coyotes scavenge garbage and will also prey on cats and small dogs.

Coyotes are active both day and night. The young are born in the spring and food requirements of the nursing females and growing young are very high at this time. By late summer, the pups are learning to hunt for themselves. It is during this time that the potential for conflict with people and their dogs increases, since dogs and their owners are generally spending more time outdoors. Coyotes are rarely, if ever, a risk to people. In the very few incidents where a coyote has bitten a human, the coyote has generally been fed by well-meaning but misguided individuals and so lost its natural fear of people. Coyotes are curious but timid animals and will generally flee if challenged. Feeding coyotes can cause

My dog is so smart, when I asked him what the economy is like, he answered: "Ruff! Ruff!"

them to lose their natural fear of people and become dependent on handouts.

Coexistence

Trapping coyotes in the city is difficult. Poisoning programs that could be employed to reduce the population would also kill other wild animals such as raccoons and squirrels, and would be a risk to dogs and children. It is not surprising that these methods are socially unacceptable.

Relocation programs also have drawbacks:

1. After removing one coyote, another (or possibly two) may move into that habitat.
2. Relocated coyotes may be at risk if they are released into an area already occupied by a coyote.
3. Relocating is simply moving the problem into someone else's backyard.

Coexistence with coyotes seems to be the best option since the coyote is difficult to trap and eradication/relocation programs in other parts of North America have proven to be both ineffective and expensive.

What can dog-owners do to co-exist with coyotes? Here are some suggestions:

1. Keep dogs under your control, and put them on a leash when walking them.
2. If you must let your dog out unattended, provide a secure space for it (such as an enclosed run).
3. Never feed coyotes. Our best defense is not to habituate them and to keep them wild.
4. Be careful not to feed coyotes unintentionally. They are attracted to:
   - improperly contained garbage
   - open composts containing fruit or vegetables
   - fallen tree-fruit
   - an overflowing bird feeder (they'll eat the grain as well as the small mammals it attracts)
   - dog food (never leave dog food outdoors)
5. Fencing helps discourage coyotes from entering your yard. Make sure fences are flush to the ground and in good repair.

Q: What did the dog say when he bumped into a tree?

A: Bark!

A Fed Coyote is a Dead Coyote

Coyotes are industrious animals, quite capable of surviving in the city without our help. In fact, by feeding coyotes you put yourself and the coyote at risk. A coyote that becomes dependent on humans for food may become too bold, lose its natural fear of people, bite someone and then have to be destroyed. (Rabies has never been detected in the BC coyote population and is therefore not a concern.) So remember: Don't feed any wildlife, especially coyotes — enjoy them safely from a distance, and they will keep their distance.

For more information on coyotes in the Lower Mainland, consult the pamphlets available from the SPCA, the City of Vancouver (Ministry of Environment) and in many vet clinics. A video on coyotes is available through the British Columbia SPCA, the Ministry of Environment and the Urban Wildlife Foundation. As well, Kristine Webber, coordinator of the Urban Coyote Project, gives community talks and can be reached by e-mail at: kwebber@unixg.ubc.ca.

LOST DOGS

Finding Your Lost Dog

— *British Columbia SPCA*

Here are tips to help you find a lost dog:
- Walk or drive through your neighbourhood several times a day, especially early in the morning and at dusk. Ask neighbours and their children (kids often know more about the neighbourhood than working parents), letter carriers, joggers, garbage collectors, newspaper carriers and others to look out for your dog.
- Go to animal shelters and the animal pound. Arrange to visit the shelters in your area rather than phoning them. Shelters may have many animals that match the description of your dog and workers are often too busy to handle phone calls. Visit the shelter every 24 hours. If you don't have a shelter in your area, contact the local police.
- Try the power of scent. Place a recently worn piece of clothing outside your door. Animals have a keen sense of smell and familiar smells can bring them home.
- Put up eye-catching posters. Distribute flyers in as many public places as you can think of: grocery stores, community centres, churches, schools, dog stores, animal groomers' and so on. If possible, include a picture of your dog. Describe your dog in detail and include your dog's name. Also include the date and place it was lost and a phone number where you can be reached. Mention any particular markings and the colour of your dog's collar. Consider offering a nominal reward. (Beware of callers who say they have your dog and demand you send them money for the animal's return. Withhold one of your dog's identifying characteristics so you can verify the honesty of the caller.)
- Place an ad in the "lost" column of local newspapers. Since many papers allow people to put in "found" ads for free, check newspapers daily in case someone is trying to find you!

- Contact "Animal Find" organizations. Some communities have non-profit groups that have formed a network to assist people who have lost a dog. When you visit your animal control shelter, ask if such a network exists in your area. Try looking in the newspaper classified ads for these groups, or ask at a dog store. If you use one of these services, remember to give a donation so they can continue to help others. Some of these groups may charge a nominal service fee.

- Check animal hospitals and vet clinics. If your dog was injured, it may have been taken to a nearby veterinarian or animal hospital before being taken to an animal shelter.

- Remember that it is far more likely that your dog has strayed from home than been stolen. If you have evidence that leads you to believe your dog was stolen, contact police and the SPCA or animal control agency. Permanent identification in the form of tattooing or a microchip implant can help authorities track your animal. Many vets believe that a combination of tattooing and microchip provides the best identification.

- Don't give out your dog's tattoo number when you advertise for your missing animal.

- Find someone who is hooked up to the Internet to post a notice about your missing dog.

- Keep a scrapbook on your dog and put in a good, recognizable photo every month when it is a puppy and at least once every six months when it is grown. If you ever lose your dog, you can take the scrapbook to a copy place to make posters.

Most of all: Don't give up! Continue to search for your dog even when there is little hope. Some animals have been lost for months before being reunited with their owners.

For a list of contacts for finding lost dogs in the Lower Mainland, see the shelters and pounds list in "Adopting from Animal Shelters" (page 38).

A lady phones a dog-food store and asks if they have coats for dogs.

"What size do you want?"

"Oh, just medium," she says.

"No, you have to measure from the top of the neck to the tail."

"Oh, I can't do that," she says, horrified. "It's meant to be a surprise!"

ID Your Dog

— British Columbia SPCA

Most dogs that end up at the SPCA have no identification, and they could easily be returned if they did. Be sure your dog is wearing up-to-date identification tags at all times. Include the dog's name and the phone numbers where owners can be reached. Most of all: Do it today! Identification tags are inexpensive. Remember, if your dog has a collar and identification, strangers will be more likely to step in and aid your lost animal.

Q: What did the owner say when his dog jumped over the fence?

A: Dog-gone.

In addition to acquiring a collar and tags for your dog, consider having it tattooed. This can be done at the same time that your dog is spayed or neutered. All SPCA shelters and most veterinarian clinics have scanners for microchips and implants. FIDO also maintains a Tattoo Tracing Service through which lost dogs can be traced and returned to their rightful owners. Calls for assistance are received from people throughout British Columbia as well as the others areas of Canada and the Western United States. Thousands of dogs (as well as cats and rabbits) have been traced since this service was established by FIDO in 1974. The service can be accessed by dialling: (604) 681-1929.

III. Caring For Your Dog

Now that you understand the rules, regulations and generally acceptable etiquette of city life with a dog, it is time to address concerns about day-to-day care. Your veterinarian and dog-owning friends are great sources of information about food and supplies. Pet supply store employees often know alot as well — so just ask. Remember that every dog's needs are different — you might find that a cooling mat is just what your "hot" dog needs, while your other dog needs a good warm coat. I'm pleased to say that, in researching what was available, I found lots of wonderful locally produced goods.

When it comes to finding a groomer, ask others with dogs of your breed for recommendations and read the West Professional Dog Groomers Association statement. The same guidelines apply to choosing a vet; the BC Veterinarian Association offers some tips as well. Traditional veterinarian medicine has much to offer your pooch, and so do many of the alternative methods of health care listed here.

Finally, at the end of this chapter you'll find information on cemetaries, cremation, headstones, grief counselling and memorials. Many of these places can help with the healing process. You'll also find a section on "immortalizing your dog" which directs you to the many talented portrait photographers and artists who specialize in capturing the living spirit of your dog.

DOG FOOD & SUPPLIES

Here is a list, by area, of places in the Lower Mainland to buy dog food and other supplies.

Burnaby

Arc Services
7724 Royal Oak Dr.
438-3524

Best Friend Pet Food & Supplies
7877 Kingsway
521-3616

Bosley's Pet Food Mart
6504 Hastings St.
298-0369

Bowser & Co
390 Howard St.
299-6434

Hastings Pet Aquariums
4233 Hastings St.
299-1666

King Ed Pet Centre
7377 Kingsway
525-4955

Korion Natural Pet Products
3999 North Fraser Way
438-2277

Middlegate Fish Bowl
408 - 7155 Kingsway
522-2035

Noah's Pet Ark
4820 Kingsway
437-3822

Pet Habitat
2174 - 4700 Kingsway
436-3080

Vancouver Pet Centres
4371 Hastings St.
294-8933

Coquitlam

Appetites Pet Food & Accessories
A4 - 1020 Austin St.
939-7299

Bosley's Pet Food Mart
3 - 2565 Barnet Hwy.
469-7893

Bosley's Pet Food Mart
329 North Rd.
939-0456

K & K Pet Foods
435 North B.A. Rd.
936-9819

Delta

Bosley's Pet Food Mart
11961 - 82nd Ave.
591-1013

Petcetara
1565 Cliveden Ave.
Annacis Island
526-4180

Pets-R-Us
1304 - 56th St.
Tsawwassen
943-0908

South Delta Pet Foods
1507 - 56 St.
Tsawwassen
943-3654

Spike's Pet Foods 'N
Stuff
6447 - 120th St.
599-0667

Ladner
Bosley's Pet Food Mart
4857 Elliott St.
946-1211

Claypool's Pet Edibles
5212 Ladner Trunk Rd.
940-1011

Perky's Pet Palace
5052 - 48th Ave.
946-8608

Langley
Best Of Friends
Enterprises (and self-
serve dog wash)
107 - 20611 Fraser Hwy.
St. Andrew's Plaza
533-3439

Buckerfield's
6000 - 200th St.
534-4135

Claypool's Pet Edibles
6183 - 200th St.
534-5511

Country Feeds
116 - 9295 198th St.
888-1449

Grover's Pet Supplies
20995 - 88th Ave.
888-7460

K & K Pet Foods Ltd
405 - 8840 210th St.
888-0116

Petfare
4042 - 200th St.
534-1424

Petfare
302 - 20771 Langley By-pass
534-6000

Total Pet Superstore
100 - 19860 Langley By-pass
534-9400

Waldo & Tubbs Pet
Food & Supplies
9110 Glover St.
888-2235

Maple Ridge
Bosley's Pet Food Mart
22745 Dewdney Trunk Rd.
463-3855

Great White Pet &
Supply Ltd
1 - 20691 Lougheed Hwy.
465-0006

Kritters Pets Ltd
145 - 22255 Dewdney
Trunk Rd.
463-7387

Buckerfield's feed stores hold annual dog washes to raise money for the SPCA. Volunteers from the SPCA wash dogs for donations of money or food. Call the Buckerfield's in your area to find out locations and dates.

Maple Ridge Pet Foods
102 - 20110 Lougheed
   Hwy.
460-0711

Ridge Feed & Pet
Supplies
22716 Dewdney Trunk
   Rd.
467-2616

New Westminster
Oakridge Pet Supplies
158 - 610 6th St.
526-6982

Perky's Pets, New West
989 Carnarvon St.
526-3300

North Vancouver
Bosley's Pet Food Mart
133 East 14th St.
984-7133

Claypool's North Shore
Pet Food
1264 Marine Dr.
988-2150

For Pet's Sake
168 - 3650 Mt Seymour
   Pkwy.
924-2455

Koko's Gourmet Pet
Food Service
no retail outlet
980-5224

Lonsdale Pet Boutique
1 - 820 Marine Dr.
987-8711

Lynn Valley Pet Foods
1266 Lynn Valley Rd.
988-9912

Paw Prints Pet Food
401 N. Dollarton Hwy.
924-0845

Paws & Claws Pantry
3071 Woodbine Dr.
984-7855

Paws & Claws Pantry
1644 Bridgman Ave.
983-2706

Pet Food 'N More
745-333 Brooksbank Ave.
980-0669

Pet Habitat
1199 Lynn Valley Rd.
986-4812

Port Coquitlam
K & K Pet Foods
23 - 2755 Lougheed Hwy.
464-5133

Mr Pet's
2879 Shaughnessy St.
464-7676

Prairie Pet Foods &
Supplies
1472 Prairie Ave.
942-0311

Richmond
Bosley's Pet Food Mart
150 - 8040 Garden City
278-0013

The Diners in the Kitchen

Our dog Fred
Et the bread.
Our dog Dash
Et the hash.
Our dog Pete
Et the meat.
Our dog Davy
Et the gravy.
Our dog Toffy
Et the coffee.
Our dog Jake
Et the cake.
Our dog Trip
Et the dip.
And — the worst,
From the first, —
Our dog Fido
Et the pie-dough.
       — James Whitcomb Riley

Bosley's Pet Food Mart
140 - 8180 No. 2 Rd.
274-3353

Companion Pet Foods
& Supplies
130 - 6280 No. 3 Rd.
821-0054

Pacific Pet
3 - 7571 Alderbridge
   Way
303-0076

Richmond Pet House
1160 - 4380 No. 3 Rd.
278-6532

Steveston Pet Food &
Supplies
140 - 12031 1st Ave.
275-5665

Tisol Pet Food
Supermarkets
5431 No. 3 Rd.
276-2254

Surrey

Aqua Terra Pets
216 - 7093 King George
   Hwy.
Newton Square Plaza
596-7662

Aqua Terra Pets
10151 King George Hwy.
Surrey Place Mall
585-1212

Bosley's Pet Food Mart
15428 Fraser Hwy.
589-4211

Bosley's Pet Food Mart
3 - 13890 104th Ave.
951-1565

Claypool's Pet Edibles
5712 - 176A St.
576-9543

Guildford Pet Foods &
Supplies
15585 - 104th Ave.
588-4115

K & K Pet Foods Ltd
125 - 15280 101st Ave.
581-5266

K & K Pet Foods Ltd
9522 - 120 St.
584-2133

Kramer's Pet World Ltd
1894 Guildford Town
   Centre
581-5888

Pet Food 'N More
400-7380 King George
   Hwy.
591-5921

Petland
102 - 19475 Fraser Hwy.
530-7878

Pets Agree
4 - 19349 94 Ave.
882-7505

Pets First Products &
Services
11824 - 78 Ave.
1-800-738-7178

Mallard Books in Richmond has a poster in the window declaring it a "dog-friendly store" and they give out doggie biscuits. Janice Barnes, the owner, figures she knows the names of all of her customers' dogs as well as she knows the names of their children.

Tisol Pet Food
Supermarkets
10616 King George Hwy.
585-3737

Wagging Tails Pet
Supplies
107 - 16033 108th Ave.
582-1680

Vancouver
Aqua Terra Pets
105 - 370 E. Broadway
873-8212

Aquariums West
1188 Davie St.
669-9249

Bosley's Pet Food Mart
1683 Davie St.
688-4233

Bosley's Pet Food Mart
4635 Arbutus St.
266-6776

Bosley's Pet Food Mart
5605 Dunbar St.
266-2667

Bosley's Pet Food Mart
6914 Victoria Dr.
327-3676

Buckerfield's
6295 Fraser St.
327-2927

Elk Creek Feed Home
Delivery
2400 - 555 W. Hastings
685-9540

False Creek Pet Supplies
104 - 1500 W. 2nd Ave.
731-2152

Granville Pet Food &
Supplies
7994 Granville St.
264-1866

K & K Pet Foods
4595 Dunbar St.
224-2513

Dog bowls by
Karen Hall

Mark's Pet Stop
1875 Commercial Dr.
255-4844

**Multiplex Aquarium
and Pet Supplies**
2347 E. Hastings St.
251-6022

Noah's Pet Ark
2886 W. Broadway
736-9517

Pawsitively Pets
1905 W. 1st Ave.
739-7297

Pet Care Centre
4364 W. 10th Ave.
228-1714

Pet Food 'N More
3669 W. 10th Ave.
731-5907

**Tisol Pet Food
Supermarkets**
6 - 2949 Main St.
873-4117

**Riplees Ranch Feed &
Pet Supply**
208 - 1670 W. 8th Ave.
736-4971

West Vancouver
Bosley's Pet Food Mart
2477 Marine Dr.
926-8841

Noah's Pet Ark
2038 Park Royal South
922-3822

**Royal Pet Foods &
Supplies**
1846 Marine Dr.
922-3071

**Village Pet Food 'N
More**
5323 Headland Dr.
925-3334

White Rock
Critters Pet Supplies
1712 - 152nd St.
535-8278

**Mother Hubbard's Pet
Foods & Supplies**
5 - 1812 152nd St.
536-6624

**Neighbourhood Pet
Food & Supply**
1625 - 128th St.
535-1399

White Rock Pets
1403B Johnston St.
531-6633

Barb Flack at Bosley's on Dunbar started the annual "Dog Photo with Santa" tradition that has spread all over the Lower Mainland. Usually Santa shows up the first weekend of December — call your favourite pet food shop for details.

SPCA Thrift Stores

The SPCA Thrift Stores give a percentage of their sales to the Vancouver Regional Branch of the SPCA. They accept donations of used goods at all locations.

Broadway Thrift Store
3626 W. Broadway
Vancouver
736-4136

New Westminster Thrift Store
1115 - 6th Ave.
New Westminster
540-7722

North Vancouver Thrift Store
1523 Pemberton Ave.
North Vancouver
983-9522

Richmond Thrift Store
5400 Minoru Blvd.
Richmond
276-2477

Cuisine for Dogs

Audley's Choice Organic Star Doggy Treats
Audley's Choice Organic Star Doggy Treats are the creation of Patty and Potsie's Organics. Patty is a former yuppie Toronto businessperson who moved to Vancouver, got a dog, started cooking for him — and a business was born. Bone-hard to clean dog's teeth, these healthy treats are loaded with good stuff: kamut, rice flour, oats and hemp seed. They sell in health food stores and hemp stores as well as a few dog food stores.

Chef Canine's School of Dog Cuisine

North Vancouver's Moneca Litton, author of *The Doggie Biscuit Book: How to Make Naturally Tasty Treats for your Dog* (Chef Canine Publishers), offers classes in dog cuisine. In three levels of instruction, Chef Canine's School of Dog Cuisine will teach you how to make nutritious dog food, tasty treats for good dogs, and birthday cakes and goodies for other party occasions. Take all three and get a certificate. Call 985-7533.

The Dog's Kitchen

The Dog's Kitchen is a 30-minute teaching video, developed in the lower mainland, on cooking for your dog. For more information, call 738-DOGS (3647) or check out the website at http://clever.net/chrisco/kitchen/dogskit.html.

Liver Treats

Recommended by trainer Marion Postgate, these liver treats can be used for dog training (please note that they are not a balanced dog food). The cookies are slightly soft when cooked, break into tiny bits easily, and do not stain clothing when put in pockets. They do go hard, or grow "fur" after 24 to 48 hours out of the freezer, since they contain no preservatives. Here's the recipe:

1 pound raw liver (ground chicken can be used)
1 raw egg
1 cup corn meal
1 to 1½ cups flour, depending on preference regarding firmness of cookies (adding a few aniseeds may increase tastiness)

Mix liver and egg in a blender or food processor until liquid. Add corn meal and flour and mix into a dough. Pat out in a pan lined with foil or wax paper, to about ⅜ inch thickness (dough will be sticky and messy). Score into 1 to 2 inch squares. Bake in oven at 350 degrees for approximately 20 minutes. (The house will smell of liver, so choose your timing well!) Remove from oven, cool, peel off paper, and break into squares. Store in a plastic bag in the freezer, and take out each cookie as required. The cookie will thaw within several minutes.

The questionable cure for a hangover to take "a hair of the dog that bit you" derives from the ancient belief that the burnt hair of a dog was an antidote to its bite.

Dog Gifts & Special Items

The following products are marketed in a number of different ways. You'll see many of these folks at the dog shows, some put their products in retail stores and some do business by mail too. If you're interested in a product, call them and ask how to get hold of it.

Animal Tracks Imports
Langley
534-9770 or 1-800-451-6596
Breed-specific gifts and collectibles, including , T-shirts and "The Springer" for biking with your dog.

Basket Arte
Vancouver
294-3522
Gift baskets for dogs — goodies in an edible basket. Edibles include bone-shaped cookies, hot dog treats, lollipops, small balls, waffles and miniature tacos.

Bitches Britches for All Seasons
Abbotsford
859-0873
Custom fitted britches, jock straps, cumberbunds and more for all breeds from Chihuahua to Mastiff.

Canine Equipment: The Ultimate Gear Fer Dogs
West Vancouver
926-9288
Utility collars, traffic leashes, Martingale training collars, fleece trail vests, fleece roll-up blankets, fleece reflective bandanas, waterproof trail dishes.

The Cat and Dog Shop
2637 W. 4th Ave.
Vancouver
733-3390
A neighbourhood pet boutique. Giftware, clocks, rubber stamps, dishes, leashes, collars, toys, natural food and supplements.

Coming and Going Designs
White Rock
535-3519
Sweatshirts of different breeds — front and back (coming and going!), tote bags, aprons, mugs, notecards etc.

Damask Designs Inc.
3600 W. 4th Ave.
Vancouver
739-6887
Floor mats, mugs, tankards, key chains, jewellry, picture frames, lightswitch plates, throws, cards, magnets, clocks, dog biscuit kits, fashion tags, books and more. Also feature Steve Hall's ceramic dogs in cars.

Dog Cross Natural Products Ltd.
Richmond
272-4198
website: http://www.eucm.org/sinobiology/dogcross/dogcross.html
Natural relief for skin allergies and arthritis. Chinese herbal wisdom provides effective, 100 percent natural alternative.

Hand-made Leather Goods
Vancouver
327-9777
Dog leashes and collars.

Holesome Pet Supplies
Port Coquitlam
944-9427
website: http://www.holesome.com/holesomekennels/
Leads, collars, flyball collars and harnesses.

ICE Fashionable Accessories
640 Hornby St.
Vancouver
682-7467
Pet lover's emporium — beautiful gifts for dog fans, including jewellry, dog bowls, frisbees, cool collars and leads, pet albums, books, beds, mats, the George line of dog gifts and more seasonal gifts.

Sally walked into her living room and saw her brother playing chess with their dog.

"Amazing!" she sputtered. "This must be the smartest dog in the history of the world!"

"He's not so smart," her brother mumbled. "I've beaten him three out of five games so far."

Invisible Fencing of Vancouver
Vancouver
878-1738
Keep your pet on your property through a combination of radio signals and Pavlovian conditioning.

Line-A-Trunk by Rear Gear
Vancouver
420-8855
Got a sport utility vehicle and a muddy, sandy or shedding dog? These liners are made of a variety of colours of Cordura nylon, custom fit for your car or truck and easy to remove and wash.

Lulu Island Designs
119 - 3800 Bayview St.
Steveston Landing
Steveston
275-5858
Dog T-shirts.

Nature's Vision Natural Health Care Products for Pets
Whalley
581-9663
Books, flower essences, herbs, homeopathics, seminars, supplements and more.

Needs n Desires Show Dog Supplies
Vancouver
869-7605
Just sell at dog shows. All the leashes, grooming products and supplies for showing your dog. Call and ask where they'll be next.

Odds n Ends
Vancouver
879-6009
Elevated feeding stations for dogs developed from an idea of the vets for guide dogs in San Rafael. Elevated feeding stations are healthy because food raised to chest level takes the stress off the skeletal body. Improves appetite, helps with hip dysplasia, arthritis and bloat. Customized for your pet.

Pridmores Custom Ceramics and Woodwork
Delta
943-1694
Stamps, spoons, keychains, prints, dishes, magnets, thimbles, mugs, grooming scissors, stationery, decals.

Redmeath Enterprises
Abottsford
859-3949
Body-cooler products, including crate or mats with a cooling filling made from a non-toxic polymer crystal. Big with Flyball fanatics to cool down their dogs. Also, cooling bandanas and body wraps for over-heated dogs.

SPCA (various branches; see listing page 38)
Cards, calendars and umbrellas — a breed umbrella and one adorned with cartoon dogs and the saying, "Raining Cats and Dogs."

Star Pets Only
275 - 2083 Alma St.
221-1891
Vancouver
Natual foods and unique gifts. Beside the Amherst Veterinary Clinic.

Tuskayla Pet Safety Gear
Vancouver
263-6167
Reflective safety vests, bands, leashes and dog backpacks.

Visi-Pet Flashing Dog Collar
Vancouver
683-8850
This collar lets you see your dog across a football field in the pitch dark.

Visually Speaking
White Rock
538-1273
e-mail: visually_speaking@bc.sympatico.ca
Dog figurines, limited edition artwork, collectibles, mouse pads, mugs, wind chimes, Christmas ornaments.

"I like dogs very much indeed...They never talk about themselves, but listen to you while you talk about yourself, and keep up an appearance of being interested in the conversation. They never say unkind things. They never tell us of our faults 'merely for our own good.'"
— Jerome K. Jerome, *Three Men In A Boat*

GROOMING YOUR DOG

Beautifying Your Beast

— *Western Professional Dog Groomer's Association*

A group of Lower Mainland dog groomers have banded together to form the Western Professional Dog Groomers Association (WPDGA). Tired of the poor image with which groomers in general have been burdened due to the negligence of an under-qualified few, these professionals are united by their common goal: to upgrade the standards of the profession and to give pets high-quality care. They subscribe to a very strict code of ethics, attend meetings every two months and have educational seminars at least once a year, thus continuously expanding their knowledge of grooming techniques. Only groomers who are members of the WPDGA are allowed to display the logo or to use the association's name in any advertising.

WPDGA members are trained professionals who can make your canine friend a happier, healthier pet that is pleasant to have around. When your groomer has your dog on her table, she will go over him from one end to the other as part of the grooming process. She is often the first to notice any changes in your pet's condition — changes which are easily overlooked in your day-to-day relationship. She will note any lumps or bumps that weren't there last time, any change in weight or coat condition, anything she feels should be brought to your attention

Photograph by
Victor Dezso

and perhaps be checked by your veterinarian. Groomers will notice warning signs such as unusual odours from the ears or mouth. Early treatment of such ailments help ensure a longer and healthier life for your pet.

A WPDGA groomer will take care of any pesky little creatures that may wish to inhabit your pet, although she cannot eliminate these pests from your house, your yard or your neighborhood. For this very important aspect of flea control she will be happy to make suggestions. She will make your pet cooler in the summer by removing excess coat, either by trimming or removing dead undercoat. In the harsher winter months, professional grooming will help ensure your pet's warmth; a well-brushed coat provides the air pockets required for proper insulation against the cold.

A well-groomed dog has no irritating little hairs brushing against the eyes causing tearing and discomfort; it has no hair and wax build-up in its ears to give bacteria a place to grow. The dog is good to be around because it looks and smells its best. While the groomer's responsibility is to do her job well, it is the owner's responsibility to have the job done regularly. If a pet is allowed to become knotted and tangled between visits, the grooming experience will not be a pleasant one. Some minor pain is bound to result. The average pet should be brushed daily and groomed professionally every four to eight weeks. A discussion with your groomer will determine what is right for your pet. Remember: A well-groomed pet is happier, healthier and certainly much more pleasant company than his ungroomed counterpart.

Irene Robinson, owner of Emma, a Keeshond (read: very hairy dog) can't say enough about Brent, the owner of Dunbar Vacuum, who besides being a serious dog owner, takes pity on fixing the vacuums of owners of shaggy dogs like Emma.

Grooming Services

Many veterinarian offices offer dog grooming, and many grooming salons also provide daycare, boarding services and training. Some companies will provide a pick-up and delivery service. Groomers will often specialize in certain breeds. Call around to find the best service for your needs and your dog's fur. The following are listings of groomers, by area:

I've got a dog as thin as a
rail,
He's got fleas all over his
tail;
Every time his tail goes
flop,
The fleas on the bottom all
hop to the top.

— Anonymous

Aldergrove
Aldergrove Kennels
26306 - 56th Ave.
664-1551 or 856-DOGS
Fax on demand:
856-5554 ext. 5000

**Puppy Trax Pet
Grooming**
27099 - 8th Ave.
857-0824

Burnaby
**Aberdeen Animal
Hospital**
4856 E. Hastings St.
293-1294

Bowser and Co.
390 Howard Ave.
299-6434

U-Wash Centre
Burnaby Veterinary
   Hospital
2210 Springer St.
299-0688

Clippers Pet Grooming
7877 Kingsway
520-6262

Glady's Doggy Salon
3849 Hastings St.
298-3544

Haute Dog
4708 Hastings St.
299-2990

**Sunnyslope Dog
Grooming**
7724 Royal Oak Ave.
454-1144

Cloverdale
**Bow-Wow-Meow Dog &
Cat Grooming**
18856 - 58th Ave.
576-0421

Coquitlam
**Chien Chic Grooming
Salon**
G-931 Brunette Ave.
521-5322

**Pet-Chien's Dog & Cat
Grooming & Supplies**
3 - 555 Clarke Ave.
936-0878

Success Dog Grooming
1022 Ridgeway Ave.
936-6422

TLC Grooming
26 - 2773 Barnet Hwy.
945-1088

Delta
**Fishworld Pets &
Supplies and Dog
Grooming**
109 - 8115 120th St.
594-3099 and 599-1559

Katie's Poodle Villa
11971 86th Ave.
590-1714

Studio One
5669 12th Ave.
Tsawwassen
943-7812

Ladner
Allbreed Dog Grooming
5126 N. Whitworth Cr.
946-6157

On The Spot Pet Grooming
5040 - 48th Ave.
940-0009

Langley
Bark Ave Canine Coiffures
105B - 20270 Industrial
    Ave.
534 -6252

Langley Dog Grooming Salon
103 - 20596 56th Ave.
534-1477

Maple Ridge
Canine Connection
22346 Lougheed Hwy.
463-7422

Country Meadows Pet Hospital
16 - 20691 Lougheed
    Hwy.
460-1428

Dog-Gone Grooming Salon
11240 - 206th St.
460-0878

San-Al's Dog Grooming Salon
11759 Fraser St.
463-8011

Zelda's Doggie World
11958 - 228th St.
467-1755

New Westminster
Carousel Cat & Dog Grooming
309 Cedar St.
526-1224

Tiffany's Doggy Salon
29 - 8th Ave.
526-5026

North Vancouver
Dogs and Company
199 Queens Rd.
986-1309; 649-4387 (cell)

Four Paws Only
734 Marine Dr.
984-8078

The Grooming Place
103 - 814 West 15th St.
984-6872

Success Dog Grooming
1912 Lonsdale Ave.
987-2333

Top Dog Groomers
3725 Delbrook Ave.
986-8341

The dog fountain at Ambleside is inscribed: "In Honour of MacDog and Arturo, pets of Lyla Bessner, May 8, 1993."

Port Coquitlam
Poco Dog & Cat Grooming
105 - 2540 Mary Hill Rd.
941-9944

Countryside Kennels
558 Prairie Ave.
945-0125

Port Moody
Diamond in the Ruff
417 Culzean Place
936-7981

Richmond
Aberdeen Kennel & Cattery Ltd.
7300 No. 5 Rd.
273-3022

Alabon Country Kennels
20391 Westminster Hwy.
270-2822

Belle Mode Boarding Kennels
6480 No. 7 Rd.
278-1354

Doggy-Six Grooming & Pet Supplies
165 - 3900 Steveston Hwy.
271-2525

Grooming With Love
190 - 8351 Alexandra Ave.
273-6444

Pampering Pets
7866 Williams Ave.
241-0130

Penny's Dog Grooming
2 - 8671 No. 1 Rd.
272-5095

Richmond Dog Grooming Studio
135-8040 Garden City Rd.
270-3013

Rondivills
16640 Westminster Hwy.
278-7181

Surrey
Animal Haven Grooming & Pet Supplies
109 - 14666 64th Ave.
597-0415

Mastergroomer: Anita's Poodle Hut
9769 - 129A St.
589-5243

Blue Ribbon Pet Supplies & Grooming
220 - 15355 24th Ave.
531-2311

Brenda's Dog Grooming
15180 Fraser Hwy.
589-5859

Dawgs & Katz
9478 - 120 St.
581-1646

Four Paws Grooming
10918 - 144th St.
951-9937

Frank's Dog & Suds
Grooming Salon
15026 Ashby Place
597-7106

Golden Hands Pet
Grooming
10432 - 156 St.
588-8809

Juanita's Doggy Den
Salon
2106 - 128th St.
538-5433

Jodi's Pet Grooming
15045 - 66A Ave.
572-3844

Groom-Rite Dog and
Cats
7070 - 144th St.
591-6252

Meadow View Acres
4044 - 184th St.
574-2323

North American Guard
Dog & Kenneling
Services
16238 - 56th St.
574-9757

Pets Beautiful
1 - 13672 108th Ave.
951-2547
e-mail:
petsbeautiful@serix.com

Pro-Tec Dog & Cat
Grooming
14715 - 108th Ave.
581-7121

Stacey's Dog Grooming:
Your Home or Mine
12911 Carluke Cr.
594-2139

Success Dog Grooming
9512 - 120th St.
585-4585

Sutton Dog Grooming
17584 - 56A Ave.
574-5373

The Ultimate Pet
Grooming Experience
12372 - 116 Ave.
580-5001

Wags & Whiskers Pet
Grooming
8948 - 157th St.
583-1208

West Coast Canine
Services
13380 - 96th Ave.
588-1317

Vancouver
Ancient Mariner Dog
Grooming
1434 E. 57th Ave.
325-6422

The Dirty Dog
3428 W. Broadway
733-9274

"Every six months David
from A Natural Pest Biz
(871-0349) comes to the
house, does his thing with
a harmless compound, and
we haven't had any fleas at
all. And we have a number
of dogs and two cats."
— Natasha Betancor-Leon,
SPCA Youth Program

93

A bloke goes to the vet to pick up his sick dog. The vet comes in with the dog and says: "I'm really sorry but I'm going to have to put your dog down."

The bloke is completely horrified and says with tears in his eyes: "WHY?"

The vet replies: "Because it's getting heavy!!"

Dog 'N Suds On Victoria
7059 Victoria Dr.
323-0448

Fraserview Animal Clinic
7291 Fraser St.
324-1523

The Grooming Shop at the SPCA
1205 E. 7th Ave.
879-7376

Happy Tails Dog Grooming Salon
3357 W. 4th Ave.
737-0042

Hollywood North Canine Training & Talent Agency
107 - 2091 W. 2nd Ave.
738-1568

Kerrisdale Veterinary Hospital
5999 W. Blvd
266-4171

Jennifer's Pet Grooming
1649 W. Broadway
733-1144

Launderdog
1064 Davie St.
685-2306

Lil' Hobos Dogs & Cats Grooming
4278 Main St.
874-6914

Obedience Plus
3387 Kingsway
435-5505

100% Pet Care
203 E. 6th Ave.
879-0077

Point Grey Veterinary Clinic
4362 W. 10th Ave.
228-1714

Pets Beautiful By Jeannine
5589 Dunbar St.
261-5310

Trudy's Dog Grooming
4051 MacDonald St.
732-7020

Vancouver Veterinary Hospital
1541 Kingsway
876-2231

Westside Pets Club
247 - 2083 Alma St.
228-1833

West Vancouver

Howe Sound Pet Services
624 Park Royal North
925-9325
(covers Bowen Island)

The Village Groom Dogspa
240 - 1425 Marine Dr.
926-1915

White Rock
Doggy Den Salon
1558 Foster
536-8366

**Sunnyside Dog & Cat
Grooming**
34 - 15531 24th Ave.
535-0505

Dena's Grooming Studio
960 - 160B St.
541-2646

Mobile Dog Grooming
**Sharan's Mobile Dog
Grooming**
Cloverdale
574-9400

**Deb's Mobile Dog &
Cat Grooming**
Richmond
526-4193

**Off the Collar Dog
Groomers**
Vancouver
874-1029

**Soggy Doggy Mobile
Dog and Cat Washing
and Grooming**
215-DOGY (3649)
Donates $1 from each
wash to SPCA Vancouver.

Grooming Supplies

Excalibur Sharpening and Supply
17841 - 64th Ave.
Surrey
576-1380

Mr. Groom Pet Grooming Products
638 W. 17th St.
North Vancouver
987-0983

Grooming Schools & Associations

Pets Beautiful
13672 - 108th Ave.
Surrey
951-2547

Western Professional Dog Groomers Association
Pat: 941-9944; or Sandy: 597-0415
Newsletter: *Groomers Grapevine*

VETERINARIANS & HEALTH SERVICES

A great veterinarian and consistent care can make all the difference towards having a healthy and happy dog and a relaxed and confident dog owner. The Lower Mainland is blessed with more than 160 qualified professionals.

How to Choose a Veterinarian

Here are some tips on finding the right vet:
- Ask your friends or neighbours which veterinary clinic they use. Are they happy with the service and the level of care? Personal referrals are the most common way veterinarians get new clients.
- Ask for a recommendation from the breeder where you purchased the animal, or ask members of your breed club.
- Ask people out walking their dogs in the park about their veterinarians.
- Check around to compare prices on basic services.
- Use the phone book or contact the BC Veterinary Medical Association (266-3441) for the name of a veterinary clinic in your neighbourhood. If you can walk to your clinic, all the better.

There are a number of veterinarian specialists in the lower mainland (dentists, opthamologists, surgeons, orthodontists, dermatologists). Your veterinarian will refer you if your dog needs to see a specialist.

After-hours Emergency Care

Many veterinarians do their own after-hour calls (on your next visit ask them how they deal with emergencies), but in the lower mainland it is also common to be referred to an emergency clinic. If you are in the unfortunate situation of having to take your dog to an Emergency Clinic, call ahead (or have someone call for you, if you don't have time to spare) so that they can be ready for you, and prepared to treat your dog as efficiently as possible. The emergency clinics are:

AFTER

BEFORE

Vancouver Animal Emergency Clinic
1590 W. 4th Ave.
Vancouver
734-5104

After Hours Pet Hospital
963 Brunette Ave.
Coquitlam
525-1188

Animal Emergency Clinic of the Fraser Valley
103 - 6337 198th St.
Langley
514-1711

Pet Ambulance and Pet Transport

If you don't drive and you need to get your dog to the veterinarian, the emergency clinic, the groomers, the airport, a kennel — even if you are divorced and have shared custody — these companies specialize in moving animals arond the city safely.

Vancouver
Cheryl's Pet Taxi
240-5132
Vancouver's original pet taxi.

Kidd Kare Pet Services
329-3736
Pet taxi all over Greater Vancouver area.

The Pet Nanny
Nicole Leblanc
899-4313

Paws-itive Pet Sitters
Elizabeth McLeod
531-7803
At-home petsitting as well.

"The Bordetella vaccination against highly contagious kennel cough is a simple intra-nasal procedure which can be given with other vaccinations at your vet's office. We insist on it, and haven't had a single case of kennel cough at our day care. Most vets don't suggest the vaccination, but you should consider it if your dog plays with any other dogs."

—Ward Bingham, owner, Launderdog

Inspired by a CBC Television item on street kids, Dr. Bruce Burton of Burton Veterinary Services in Bradner (856-4166) suggested to a client who was a Vancouver street cop that maybe he could help out. Dr. Burton was particularly struck by the kids' comments that their pets were their only constant companions. With the help of Officer Warren Lemke and Street Youth Services, who get the word out, Dr. Burton puts on a clinic in downtown Vancouver about once every two months. There are often line-ups, and he can see up to 40 animals per clinic. Most often, he deals with vaccinations and minor out-patient health care. Dog food is obtained from the food bank or by donation. "The kids are more knowledgeable about their animals than I expected them to be, and care for them quite well," says Dr. Burton.

Peace of Mind Pet Services
Julie Bryson
984-7395
The ambulance goes all over the greater Vancouver area, and is called by vets or owners. Owners can ride in the car, they have oxygen and all other first aid and life-saving devices on board.

Rondivills
278-7181
Pet taxi service; also quarantine dogs coming into the country.

Rosie's Pet Services
589-4314 or 435-6160
Pet taxi, dog walking, petsitting.

Aldergrove
Valley Pet Taxi and Services
855-1419
Pet sitting, walking and tranport.

First Aid & Veterinarian Assistant Courses

Ann W. Jackson, Behaviorist and Motivational Trainer
North Vancouver
922-3851
All of Jackson's courses include emergency first aid and preventative health care.

Practical First Aid for Animals
Granville Business College
320 - 855 Dunsmuir St.
Vancouver
683-8850
This one-day course is taught by a veterinarian and offered about every three months.

Veterinary Assistant Program
Granville Business College
320 - 885 Dunsmuir St.
Vancouver
683-8850

Veterinary Office Assistant Program
Granville Business College
320 - 885 Dunsmuir St.
Vancouver: 683-8850
This six-month program covers everything from anatomy to parasites to office skills, and includes a two-day large animal workshop on Gambier Island. High demand from employers for graduates.

West Coast College of Health Care
Campuses in Surrey and Abbotsford
951-6644 or 1-800-807-8558
Six-and-one-half-month program. Program includes Animals and Animal handling, vaccinations, pesticides, computer skills and CPR, Level C.

The SPCA offers first aid courses. Call: 879-5494

Portrait by
Chris Clarke

You will fetch
many sticks

Alternative Therapies

Canine Caretakers
Evelyn Bliss
Vancouver
270-0309
Behavioural counselling and herbal consulting.

Holistic Pet Care Centre
19008 - 60A Ave.
Surrey
574-0002
website: http://www.uniserve.com/holisticpet
Skin problems, allergies, fleas and ticks, rheumatism, nutritional supplements, arthritis, home emergency kits, immune booster, tartar build-up, hair/nail promoter. In-home or centre visits.

Sidh G. Khare, Acupuncturist
320 - 10th Ave.
New Westminster
525-0647

Out of The Earth
Cynthia Rice
Vancouver
583-6993
Call for catalogue and newsletter. Often at the dog shows; uses aromatherapy, or massage with essential oils. Useful for dogs with muscle pain, arthritis and dysplasia, as well as perking them up for showing (boosting confidence and calming them down) and boosting the immune system. Flower essence therapies used for fear, aggression, depression, calming, for rescue and shelter stress and for show dog stress. Natural flea control too.

Quest Clinic Physiotherapists Corp.
Cynthia Webster
257 - 4255 Arbutus St.
Vancouver
731-1374

Reiki and Crystal Healings
Chris Poellein
Vancouver
733-7869
For pain management, speeding up healing and behavioural changes.

Renee Riel Telepathic Animal Communications
Vancouver: 583-0342
Renee communicates with animals. Wondering what your dog really thinks? Give Renee a call.

Elaine Thompson Alternative Body Worker and Pet Psychic
Vancouver
739-4854 or 1-888-878-8281
Holistic combination of bodywork including shiatsu, acupressure, acupuncture, reflexology, reiki, polarity therapy, cranial sacral therapy, aromatherapy, applied Kinesiology and muscle testing. Psychic services include behavioural problems and crisis intervention, telepathic communication with your pets, and finding lost animals. Housecalls, workshops and one-on-one classes available.

Tellington Touch Every Animal Method (TTEAM)
Myles Herman, Crystal Oak Stable
Vancouver
857-2202
This is a therapeutic touch system, originally devised for horses by Linda Tellington-Jones of California and now used successfully with many animals, including dogs.

Vancouver Homeopathic Centre for Animals
Susan Sigmund
Vancouver
687-7176
e-mail: ssigmund@ultranet.ca
Phone consultations and home visits available. Holistic pet care, homeopathic medicine, behaviour problems, non-toxic worming/flea control, nutritional counselling, and chronic disease. We use a natural flea control alternative chemical intervention.

"The very best book about dog health care is an easy-to-understand medical reference book, *The UC Davis Book of Dogs*, edited by Mordecai Siegal (Harper Collins, 1995)."
—Cathy Tweeddale, breeder of Labrador Retrievers

Health Insurance

There is only one company in Canada offering health insurance for dogs. Pet Plan Insurance is worth considering — talk to your veterinarian about expected and unexpected medical costs. Pet Plan has a number of levels of programs available.
1-800-661-7699
website: http://www.petplan.com

Care of Older Dogs

The gingham dog went
"Bow-wow-wow!"
And the calico cat replied
"Mee-ow!"
The air was littered, an
hour or so,
With bits of gingham and
calico.
— Eugene Field,
"The Duel"

Concerned dog owner Doris Orr (also of DONATE — the Doris Orr Needy Animals Trust Endowment; see page 42) has some sage advice for owners of older dogs. Orr reminds owners that older dogs can't run as fast or swim as far as they used to. Dogs can actually die if they are pushed beyond their limits. Owners should not expect their dogs to be able to run alongside a bicycle or swim into the ocean current like they once did. As dogs age, they may develop arthritis or hip problems which may affect their ability to go up and down stairs. Instead of putting dogs down, Orr suggests getting a ramp. The dogs will be able to get around more easily and you will have allowed them to live longer.

Facilities for Older Dogs
Birch-Bark Kennels
26436 - 13th Ave.
Aldergrove
856-4321
Boarding services and daycare. Also do sick and geriatic care.

Peace of Mind Pet Services
Julie Bryson
984-7395
Geriatric care and sick care in owner's home. Do hydrotherapy and physiotherapy.

IF YOUR DOG DIES

Dealing with Grief

Here are some organizations that offer support for bereaved dog owners.

Animal Grief Support of BC
Moneca Litton
985-7533
This non-profit society offers a telephone support network as well as dog prayers and funerals.

Theresa Stokowski and Associates
263-1724
Pet loss and bereavement counselling: in-person, group and telephone counselling.

People-Pet Partnership
College of Veterinary Medicine
Washington State University
(509) 335-1297
website: http://www.wsu.edu:8080/~douglasc/ppp/
    petloss.htm

The Pet Loss Support Hotline
Davis School of Veterinary Medicine, University of California
(916) 752-4200
Volunteers help with grief, or help you find support in your geographical area.

Pet Loss and Bereavement Packet
Delta Society, P.O. Box 1080
Renton, Washington
98057-9906
(206) 226-7357
This 100-page packet includes articles, brochures and a list of videos to help adults and children cope with the loss of a pet. Includes a Directory of Pet Loss Resources, $16 (plus $5 shipping and handling per packet).

Dr. Adrian Cooper's book recommendation:
Pet Loss: A Thoughtful Guide for Adults and Children, by Herbert A. Niebert and Arlene Fischer (Harper and Row).

Amanda Vaughn's Pet Loss and Bereavement (an audio tape)
P.O. Box 53590, 984 W. Broadway
Vancouver
V5Z 4M6
736-4665
This tape is like a personal counselling session.

Dog Cemeteries & Crematoria
In addition to the establishments listed below, every branch of the SPCA offers crematory services.

Occasionally you will see dog obituaries in the paper. *The Vancouver Sun* has a section in the classified ads called Pet Services/Notices.

Special Friends Pet Services
165 Riverside
North Vancouver
929-3491
Offers private and non-private cremations.

Photograph by
David Beckett

Vancouver City Pound
251-1325
Provides private cremations for dogs of Vancouver residents for $50. Non-private cremations are $15 if you bring your deceased dog to them and $25 if they have to pick it up. They also have a vet on hand to euthanize the animal. This costs $15 if the dog is delivered to them, $25 if they have to retrieve it.

Western Pet Memorial Foundation, BC Branch
11173 - 135 St.
Surrey
Concerned citizens in Surrey have formed this foundation to preserve and maintain their pet cemetery. They are trying to raise $172,000 to save this, one of only two pet cemeteries in BC. They also want to create a monument for all the province's cremated and deceased pets.

Pet Memorials
J.B. Newall Personalized Dog Memorials
5096 Fraser St.
Vancouver
327-1312
Bring in a photo of your dog and J.B Newall Memorials will engrave it in a river rock headstone, with the name of the dog, dates, and one or two lines of text. River rocks are smooth, flat rocks, 10 to 12 inches in width, taken from the rivers in the valley. Price ranges from $125 to $185 depending on the size of the stone. Stones take 3 to 4 weeks to carve and J.B. Newall will deliver the finished memorial (within the Lower Mainland).

The Companion Animal Health Fund
Western College of Veterinary Medicine
University of Saskatchewan,
Saskatoon, Saskatchewan
S7N 0W0
This fund is an ideal place to make a donation in memory of a dog who has died. The money they collect goes towards research on improving the health and care of dogs. The college also sends out a lovely notification letter in memory of the dog to the dog's owner.

When your dog or a friend's dog dies, you might consider making a donation in its memory to the SPCA or your favourite local charity.

IMMORTALIZING YOUR DOG

Dog Photography

Just because you want to capture the moment, doesn't mean you can capture the movement. Professionals can get amazing results with animals. Look for examples of their work throughout this book.

David Beckett Photography
688-6864
Black and white studio portraits of dogs (see pages 27, 30 and 104).

Heather Culliford
325-5810
Photography in natural relaxed settings (see page 137).

K.A. Davidson
601-0046
She shoots dogs — and their people (see page 13 and 110).

Photograph by
Gary Wildman

Victor Dezso Foto
430-0026
Pets, people, places and products — photography on location and in the studio (see page 88).

Ellice Hauta Photography
534-1145
Capturing the essence of your pet on location or in your home (see pages 52, 169 and 171).

Kristine Kavalec
274-2038
Acrylic, chalk or black-and-white portraits (see page 208).

Linda Lindt
980-8910
Specializing in animal photography, including most of the BC dog shows (see page 110).

Yukiko Onley
739-0429
Portraits and travel photography (see page 219).

Kent Southwell Dogumentary Photography
738-3673
Providing pet owners with fine art, documentary style portraits of their dogs. (see pages 31, 49 and 176).

Lionel Trudel
813-3434
Portraits of pets and pet people (see page 61, 232 and front cover).

Wendy Wedge
926-7452
Photography on location and in the studio (see page 19).

Wildman Photography
Put your pet into the family portrait with North Shore photographer Gary Wildman (see page 106).
988-2753

On the West Vancouver Seawall, about one kilometre west of John Lawson Park on the train-track side of the walk, there is a semi-circular indent. It contains a drinking fountain for humans at human level, and, imbedded in the masonry of the wall, a basin for dogs to drink from. Inside the basin is a concrete bone. A plaque reads: "Gabriel's Fountain, 1986."

Dog Portraits

These artists specialize in capturing the essence of dogs through various media: paint, pastels, wood carving and sculpture.

Animal Town
985-9252
Canadian clay sculptor Steve Hall can sculpt your dog in relief. Will depict dog driving your car or in realistic form (see pages 25 and 56).

Chris Clarke
541-1181
Portraits of dogs and horses (see page 99).

Kelly Davis
946-6157
Dog carvings in cedar.

Graham Eagle–Ayrie Studio
986-8649
Folk-art bird feeders, wine dispensers and utensil holders come in many doggy themes (see page 202).

Judy Fry
224-4865
Finely detailed portraits that capture your special animal's personality (see page 140).

Wendy Grossman
274-2890
Lovingly captures your dog's spirit and physicality in quality watercolour portraits (see page 140).

Michelle Leavitt
433-6538
Realistic watercolour portraits and drawings from your photographs.

There is a ground level dog drinking fountain (below the human version) prominently placed on Robson Street, in front of what was the main branch of the Public Library and is now the entrance to Virgin Records/Planet Hollywood. It reads: "Donated on Vancouver's Centennial, by Mrs. Theresa Galloway."

Leah MacFarlane
879-1872
Watercolour portraits from photographs after meeting
the "client" to read their personality (see page 181).

Julia Morton
980-5976
e-mail: morton@direct.ca
website: http://www.geocities.com/SoHo/6804
Capture your pet's personality in full colour pastel (see
page 46).

Elaine Sills
922-5490
e-mail: esills@direct.ca
Specializing in interpreting personal memories of special
pets (see page 15).

Patricia Symons Eagle Eye Intuitive Animal Portraits
525-3493
Specializing in quality animal portraits.

Dog Bowls

Karen Hall
926-8030
Personalized dishes! Your choice of blue, green or cream
for your large, medium or small dog (see page 80).

Georgina Brandon
886-3588
Sells at Granville Island Public Market every three weeks
or so (see page 213).

Cartoonists:

Sa Boothroyd (cartoonist for this book)
669-1932
Sells at Granville Island Public Market once a month and
at Sun's Place on Robson St. Her work is also at Oh
Brothers in Kerrisdale.

The cost of donating a dog
or human fountain in the
City of Vancouver is a
minimum of $2000 (all tax
deductible). The price will
vary depending upon the
proximity of the water
source. Contact Carol
DeFina at 257-8440.
Check out Fraser River Park
for an example of the first
fountain with icons
indicating "dogs drink
here."

Photograph by
Linda Lindt

Photograph by
K.A. Davidson

IV. Walking Your Dog

There are hundreds of great places in the Lower Mainland to exercise your dog. For starters, there are neighbourhood parks everywhere. At least a couple of times a day you can find great clutches of people, often with coffee mugs in hand, chatting away and visiting while their dogs play happily in these green spaces. People choose these parks because of proximity, the mix of dogs, how well the park is looked after (and how little dog doo is left by irresponsible dog owners) and, sometimes, because of the drainage. This is a rain forest, and if you have a tennis-ball dog like we do, drainage becomes even more important. Nothing like a good game of mud ball to send you searching for a school ground or park with a hard-packed playing field. Finding a spot where a ball will still bounce in a downpour becomes tantamount when you have a very active dog. As you search for that perfect place, however, be mindful of the activity schedule of schools — and pick up after your pooch.

Then there are the big walks: the trails, the edges of the Fraser River, the beach fronts and the large parks where owners can get a decent workout too. We are blessed with plenty of green space in and around Vancouver, and in all of these public areas there is a delicate relationship between dog walkers, walkers without dogs, bicyclists, skateboarders, joggers and parents with strollers. Remember: Common sense, good road sense and reliable dog-doo extraction make for happier trails all around.

A COMMUNITY OF DOG WALKERS

— Margot Kerr, Ambleside regular and owner of the remarkable Joey

"Pray tell me, sir, whose dog are you?"
— Alexander Pope

I love my dog. While I have yet to find a 12-step program to help me with this addiction, I *have* found a compassionate support group. Before I acquired my dog, I had lived in West Vancouver for just over a year and my social interaction had been limited to grocery shop cashiers and clerks at my favourite video store. A month after adopting my pup, I was recognizing people on the street and they were recognizing the lady at the end of Joey's leash. Conversations were brief and dog related, but I was starting to feel like a part of the community. I was offered advice on pet food, veterinarians and trainers, but mostly I heard about the section of Ambleside Park where dogs could "unleash" their energy.

When Joey had achieved the ripe old age of four months, and I had armed him with the essential immune boosters and an A-OK from the vet, we headed to the fabled Ambleside Park. I was nervous. What if nobody played with my pup? Should I let him off the leash? Would he come when called? That was exactly a year ago — a year measurable by the passage of puppyhood, the growing number of Joey's playmates (and the number of vets we've been through) and the sense of belonging I feel.

We've all heard about the benefits of Animal Assisted Therapy, how prisons, hospitals and long-term care facilities incorporate pets into their programs. We know that having a pet instills responsibility in children and alleviates loneliness in virtually anyone. To many of us this is simply common sense. What's not so commonly understood is the social dynamic among regulars at the local "dog beach." A process takes place that is rare and startling: the natural selection of friends through the pure instincts of our dogs.

It's not subtle, this natural selection. The first rule: Neither a nose in your groin nor drool on your pants must deter you from praising a prized pet. Over time, newcomers learn the common code of ethics, unspoken rules and appropriate attire. After your attendance (regardless of weather) has been noted for some months, other regulars will move beyond calling you "Lassie's Mum or Dad" and will learn your human name, IF: when carrying your full "doggie bag," you don't stop to shake hands; you graciously give extra bags to those in need; you "have biscuits in your pocket and are glad to see me"; your eyes never glaze over when shown pictures of pets; and, most important, you take full responsibility for your dog's behaviour.

Having passed through these stages of socialization, one day you will find yourself overwhelmed by how many people look forward to your visit. Books will be exchanged, recipes swapped and intimacies shared. Other dog walkers will fret when your dog is sick and worry when you miss a day. They may also laugh if you wear white pants or open-toed shoes. Most of all, you will have discovered one of the best networks in the world: the one that supports you when your life has gone to the dogs!

Vancouver Dog Owners Association

As this book goes to press, the Vancouver Park Board is talking with dog owners about off-leash park access. This communication was precipitated by the city enforcing the by-law that states dogs must be on leash (in the past, the City Pound did little to enforce this, particularly in parks). In May 1997, when $75 tickets were handed out in Vancouver, dog owners got vocal and got organized. A group (spearheaded by Glen Swain, who can be contacted at 736-4640) formed the Vancouver Dog Owners Association to propose some amendments to the by-law. The proposals include:

1. that dogs be allowed off the leash in the parks until 9 a.m. each morning;
2. that all larger parks have designated off-leash play areas for all times of the day;
3. that some designated beach areas be usable at any time of the day for dogs to swim.

These proposals were intended to spark dialogue and they have certainly done that. The issue is not simple: having off-leash areas for dogs is a privilege, not a right. There are thousands of dog lovers, but small children, parents, wildlife advocates and people who dislike and/or are scared of dogs also have rights that must be protected. The Park Board is listening to all sides and I am confident they will soon launch a pilot project built upon a reasonable compromise.

Each incidence of irresponsible dog ownership always reflects badly on the responsible dog owners. Catching a dog in the act of doing its business and the owner in the act of not picking it up is very difficult for the animal control people, so the only way to crack down on these irresponsible owners is for other dog owners to do the policing in a friendly but persuasive way. Gently shame them: "Did you forget your bag? I've got an extra — no problem!" is a good phrase to use.

WALKING IN THE RAIN

Essential Gear

Anyone who walks a dog knows that great wet-weather gear is essential for the Lower Mainland. Here's what a few professional dog walkers wear to battle the rain:

Adrienne Wood:
Jeans and Sugoi bicycling jacket with a hood.

Dogs and Company:
Australian outback coat and hat.

Teri Booth:
Waterproof poncho, cowboy hat, hiking boots.

I Love Dogs:
Big rubber boots, big grey raincoat, track pants under jeans and three shirts.

Heather Culliford:
Polar Fleece with rubber on top (cheap from army surplus on Broadway) and gumboots with Gortex socks.

Grizzly's Dog Walking:
"Still searching for ultimate raingear!"

Sandy Morris:
Helly Hansen jacket and running shoes.

The Dog House:
Australian outback coat.

The Purple Leash:
"I have a car full of assorted outer wear and I wear what is dry and suits the purpose."

Andrew Fawcett:
"I carry an umbrella!"

The Dog

The truth I do not stretch
  or shove
When I state the dog is full
  of love.
I've also proved, by actual
  test,
A wet dog is the lovingest.
— Ogden Nash

DOG WALKS IN THE LOWER MAINLAND

The following are suggestions for particularly great places to walk with your dog in the various municipalities in the lower mainland. We've included the comments of actual dog-owners in the area, where possible. For North and West Vancouver, all dog map information has been included because these are by far the most dog-organized municipalities.

With a few noted exceptions, dogs are to be leashed everywhere. While most folks who risk walking their dogs off leash are responsible about keeping the dogs in view, under control and picking up after them, complaints to the animal control people are usually against the dog owners who disregard these practices. We all suffer because of these few. Encouraging other dog owners to toe the line will make our city a better place for all.

> "I know Sir John will go, though he was sure it would rain cats and dogs."
> — Jonathan Swift

Burnaby

Dogs are to be on leash everywhere except the experimental areas in Robert Burnaby and Confederation Parks.

Burnaby Mountain Park

This is a harder trek, so before you tackle these trails decide who really needs the walk — you or your dog.
— Burnaby Parks Department

Deer Lake Park

Deer Lake Park in Burnaby is great. It's a good hour's walk either on trails or up the hills by the old Okalla Prison area. Lots of wide open green spaces. And the bonus is a swim at the end to clean off the mud from the trails. Watch for stinging nettles.
— Cathy Tweeddale, owner of Yellow Labs Midas and Sophie.

Fraser Foreshore Park

In South Burnaby, the Fraser Foreshore Trail at the end of Byrne Road is great. You can walk the entire distance to Boundary Way on leash. A group is working on trying to make part of it an off-leash area. There is a swimming spot at Sussex Creek. Much of the trail is great for access to the water. A group gets together every day around 4 p.m. The trail is along the river's edge — the trees are on one side and water on the other so there is no traffic. Despite the development around it, Foreshore Trail will be preserved because it belongs to Burnaby Parks.

— Sandy Curtis, owner of Gemma, a Lab-Doberman cross.

Robert Burnaby and Confederation Parks

These already popular sites are even more popular since the one-year trial off-leash areas started July 1, 1997. In Confederation Park, the off-leash area is the forested trail north of Penzance Drive. In Robert Burnaby Park, the BC Hydro right-of-way is off leash for a year. For this trial to work, dog owners have got to be responsible — any complaints about excrement not being picked up and dogs out of control will be considered when city council reviews this program in a year.

Robert Burnaby Park

Robert Burnaby Park is very dog friendly. Hang a left off the trail from the 4th Street entrance by the ball park, and there is a section where groups of folks get together every day at different times. The dogs get along very well. We help each other out by spotting for the SPCA!

— Mindy Lamont, owner of Border Collies Molly and Wrigley

Coquitlam
Coquitlam River Path

Along the Coquitlam River up towards the dam is a great place to go. There's a gravel path that leads down to the water and an area where the dogs can swim.

— Lee Oiom, owner of Akitas Turbo, Storm and Miko

Minnekhada Regional Park

Turn off the Lougheed Highway onto Coast Meridian Road and you will see the green GVRD signs leading you to a remarkable place, an oasis of nature in stark contrast to the nearby huge shopping malls and housing developments. There is a parking lot shortly before you get to the enormous Scottish-style hunting lodge, built as a retreat by Lieutenant-Governor Eric Hamber in 1934. You can tour the lodge on certain Sundays throughout

A burglar was in a dark house. When he picked up the TV a voice said, "Jesus is watching you."

He dropped the TV and whirled around, looking for someone but without any luck. He picked up the VCR and the voice said again, "Jesus is watching you."

The burglar dropped the VCR and demanded, "Who said that?"

A voice in the back of the room said, "Me, Clarence!"

He spotted a parrot and asked, "Did you say that?" Clarence acknowledged that he had. The burglar then asked, "Who would name a Parrot Clarence?"

To which Clarence replied, "The same guy who named the Rottweiler Jesus!"

the year. The view from the porch is reminiscent of looking over the Scottish moors. There are many great trails with a whole range of difficulties. You could do a good three hours if you leave the park and take the Addington Loop Trail, which goes along the dike on the marsh at the Pitt River.

— *Marg and Noel, and Rosie the Border Collie*

Mundy Park

Mundy Park has forest and bark mulch trails. It is very cool in the summer, which is great on a hot day. The trail system is very dense, and the perimeter trail is about 6 kilometres. And there is a whole dog culture in there — lots of nice people with well-behaved dogs. There are mapboards throughout the park to guide you — you could get lost — and there are two lakes in the park. The best parking is off the west side of the park on Hillcrest Street.

— *Sue Haberger, owner of Tessa, an elderly long-haired German Shepherd*

Riverview Hospital Lands

The Riverview Lands are public lands — 250 acres in total. There is a psychiatric hospital on the sloping property, with a park-like setting in front. A wonderful arboretum is located there, with a large collection of old trees and a lovely lawn. Sometimes you will meet patients out there, and if you have a friendly dog, it can be magical — the patients love to visit and the dog can provide rare moments of pleasure. Up behind the hospital (we call it the backyard) it is very rural, with meadows, old gardens and streams. A packed dirt road, suitable for bikes or strollers, runs the length of the property across the back for about 2 kilometres. The Riverview Horticultural Centre Society is trying to maintain this acreage as public space. You can access it off the Lougheed Highway or Mariner Way. There is lots of parking.

— *Sue Haberger, owner of Tessa, an elderly long-haired German Shepherd*

Riverview Park

Above the hospital lands is another park best accessed off Mariner Way, down to Chilco until you come to Mara. Turn left on Mara at the stop sign, then turn right

> "All that I have to say, is, to tell you that the lanthorn is the moon; I, the man in the moon; this thorn-bush, my thorn-bush; and this dog, my dog."
>
> — William Shakespeare, *A Midsummer-Night's Dream*

on Clearwater to the parking lot. There is a huge oval park, with a walk circling it from above. You can look down into the fields and get a clear idea of who is walking their dog towards you. I have toy dogs so I worry about bigger dogs. This is a safe place.

—Julie Beaton, owner of Della, Mr. Wiggles and Finnegan the Papillons.

Delta
The Dikes

I start at the west end of River Road and Columbia Point. That dike actually starts in Ladner and goes right around to Roberts Bank. I like the fact that most of the time I can leave my dog off-leash. We also like the dike in South Delta (south end of 64th Avenue or 72nd Avenue) around the Boundary Bay airport — it isn't too busy and there is lots of area between the dike and the water where my dog can run and not disturb the wildlife. Neither dike is muddy, which is a blessing in our weather.

— Harley Rea and Panettone the Boxer

Langley
Aldergrove Lake Regional Park

The park is located at 264th St. and 8th Ave. Dogs must be leashed. There is an off-leash area where dogs can run under the owner's control, at the northeast corner of the park off Lefeuvre Road. Dogs are not permitted in the beach area. Please remove your dog's droppings.

— Greater Vancouver Regional District

At Aldergrove Lake Regional Park there is a small off-leash field area in the northeast corner of the park. And there's a network of interconnecting trails. Some are flat, some are really hilly. You can do a half-hour to two-hour walk without re-tracing your steps. It's very private, secluded and full of vegetation, flowers and spawning fish. My pet peeve is the horrible people who have un-controlled dogs off-leash on the trails, harassing owners and properly leashed dogs, and disturbing the wildlife.

— Ann Webster, President, Lower Mainland Whippet Association. Owner of Zenobia, Panda and Vincent (Whippets), as well as E.B.G., Angel, Obsidian and eight more Greyhounds.

Passing through Chilliwack? Saturday mornings there is an organized dog walk. Meet behind the Bank of Montreal at 10 a.m. and head out on an on-lead walk with a few obedience exercises, including socializing time at a nearby playground.

Campbell Valley Regional Park

Dogs must be leashed. There are currently two off-leash areas being tested in the park along 4th Avenue. They can be reserved for canine recreation events. Please remove your dog's droppings.
— *Greater Vancouver Regional District*

Derby Reach Park at Allard Crescent

Dogs must be leashed. Please show courtesy to other park visitors by removing your dog's droppings.
— *Greater Vancouver Regional District*

Houston Trail — part of Derby Reach Park — is a nice long walk, very beautiful and peaceful. It takes about an hour.
— *Tracey Fiddler, owner of Golden Retrievers Maggie and Gypsy*

Gladwin Park

Gladwin Park has a designated dog training area. It is a modest sized park but has a small pond, so it is a great place for training dogs for water retrieving (we use tennis balls and bumpers).
— *Dennis Robbins, owner of Sundee Labradors*

Nathan Creek Dike

Where Nathan Creek crosses River Road there is a public dike which is a gorgeous trail along the river for biking, jogging and walking. There's lots of wildlife, and it is a great dog walk.
— *Dennis Robbins, owner of Sundee Labradors*

Maple Ridge

Dike Access

There is dike access at the following places:
Harris Road (at the end);
203 Street;
132nd Avenue;
28th Avenue between Laicy and 132nd Avenue.

In the town of Steveston, a friendly Irish Setter that roamed the streets for years is commemorated in the park next to the Post Office/ Museum. A plaque reads: "Big Red Forever Remembered, 1989."

Golden Ears Park

Golden Ears Park is massive and it is all trails. It is great for really big walks and there are a couple of lakes. It is horse-friendly, too.

— Jill Koch, owner of Pointers Ace, Ponty and Tri

Kanaka Creek Park

Kanaka Creek Park is a huge park that starts around the Albion Ferry and goes all the way up along Kanaka Creek to Cliff Falls, where there are picnic areas. There are walking trails and horse riding trails throughout the park. It's not too populated at the Cliff Falls end, and there are lots of dogs.

— Jill Koch, owner of Pointers Ace, Ponty and Tri

Pitt Polder Dikes

I think there should be at least a half-dozen large areas along the dikes in the Pitt Polder area for the dogs to be off leash legally. Dogs need to run, and there are a number of serious trainers who want to train their dogs in that area to be competitive (amateur and professional levels). The dikes are great for training — cover, water and distance. It is also a beautiful area; you can lose yourself out there.

— Randy Blanchard, owner of Shodan, Misty and Classy, Black Labrador Retrievers

New Westminster
Annacis Island

At the west end of Annacis Island near the new Neptune Fish Plant there is a road you can walk on all the way around the western point of the island. Recently, on the south side of that point, a bunch of ex-fishermen have been doing a beautiful job of cleaning up the tidal beach and park area. The best time to go is during the day in the week. It is a safe place and lovely.

— Cherie Holmes, breeder and owner of Doberman Pinschers Paige, Kesch and Tracy

North Vancouver

There is an excellent map available as part of the District and City of North Vancouver's "Dogs in Parks Regulations." To obtain the map, check with the SPCA or City Hall. The following information is taken from the regulations:

Dogs ARE ALLOWED throughout North Vancouver on all thoroughfares and in certain parks, provided they are on leash or, in some cases, off leash, if under control by the owners.

Dogs ARE NOT ALLOWED on playgrounds, picnic areas, playing fields, beaches, fitness circuits, running tracks, golf courses, bowling greens, tennis courts and specifically not allowed in the parks, and/or at the times, listed below.

A. Parks Where Dogs are Prohibited

City:
14th Street Mall
Bewicke
Chief August Jack
Chief Dan George
Chief Mathias Joe
Derek Inman
Eastview
Emerald
Hamersley
Heywood (playground area, playing fields)
Larson
Loutet (playing fields)
Mahon (playgrounds, picnic area, playing fields)
McDougall Field
McEvoy
Mosquito (16th & Fell)
Norseman
Ottawa Gardens
Rey Sargent

Roger Burns Green
Sam Walker
Semisch
Street Andrews
Tempe Heights playground
Tot Lot, 27th Street & 28th Street E, 200 Block
Victoria, West
Waterfront (south of BC Rail tracks)

District:
Arborlynn Park
Blueridge Park
Braemar Park
Briarlynn Park
Cleveland Park
Delbrook Park
Dudley Place
Eastview Park
Eldon Park
Evelyn Park
Fairmont Park
Fairway Park

A dog walks into an unemployment office and asks the man behind the desk if he could help him find work. The man, astonished at the sight of a speaking dog, replies, "I think I can help you." He immediately phones the circus to find out if they could use the dog in their routine. The dog overhears some of this conversation and says, "I hate to interrupt, but what would the circus want with a brick layer?"

Glenwood Park
Grousewoods Park
Indian River
Inter-River (around
    playing fields & courts)
Institute Road Tennis
    Court
Kilmer Park
Kirkstone Park
Lillooet Road Field
Lynn Valley Park
Lynnmour Tot Lot
Lynnmour
    Neighbourhood
MacGowan
Maplewood Farm
Maplewood
Marie Place Tot Lot
McCartney Creek
Michael Park
Murdo Fraser (Paisley to
    end of Elizabeth Way
    and golf course)
Myrtle Park
Norgate Park
Pioneer
Roche Point Field
Rockland Park
Russell Court
Sarita Park
Seylynn skateboard area
    and play field
Sherwood Park
Sowden Park
Strathcona Park
Strathaven Park
Trillium Park
Underwood
Viewlynn Park
Welsh Strip tennis courts
    east to Pemberton
William Griffin Park
Windsor Park

B. Parks Where Dogs are Permitted on Leash (October 1 to April 15)

City:
Eastview
Lynnmouth
Wagg

District:
Alderwood Park or
    Nortgate Strip
Belle Isle Place Park
Bridgman Park
Brooksbank Park
Carisbrooke Park
Cates Park
Deep Cove
Mackay Creek Park
Panorama Park
Seylynn Park, north of
    the community centre

C. Parks Where Dogs are Permitted on Leash

City:
Boulevard (between W.
    and E. Grand
    Boulevard)
Greenwood
Heywood (wilderness
    area)
High Place
Hyak (running water)
Loutet (dog run)
Mahon (wilderness area)
Moodyville
Sunrise
Tempe Heights
Victoria, East
Waterfront (north of BC
    Rail tracks)

Q: Did you hear about the vampire's dog?

A: It was a bloodhound!

District:
Alpine Parks
Bowser Trail between
 Capilano Road and
 Pemberton
Bridgman East Side and
 Trails
Byron Park
Capilano River Park and
 Trails (GVRD)
Doran Park
Draycott Park
Eastridge viewpoint
Eldon Park, trail around
 perimeter of park
Grousewoods Trail
Harbourview Park
Hunter Park
Inter River in
 undeveloped areas
Lynn Canyon Park
Mackay Creek between
 15th and Esplanade
McNair Park
Montroyal (Cliffridge
 Park)
Mosquito Creek
Murdo Fraser from
 Elizabeth Way to
 Crescentview Drive
Myrtle Park, trail around
 the sportsfield and
 leading to and from
 Strathcona Road
Perimeter of Roche
 Point Park
Princess Park trails
Sechelt Park
Seymour River Park
Starlight Way along the
 creek
Trail through Sarita
 Creek area

Twin Lakes Park
Walkways in the Indian
 River Park
Welch Street Strip, west
 of the tennis courts
Westover Park
Wickenden Park
William Griffin Trails
Windridge Park around
 Ron Andrews Pool

**D. Parks and Other
Areas Where Dogs are
Permitted Without
Leash but Under
Control**

City: none

District:
Powerlines
Indian River Road
Rice Lake Road north of
 Dempsey
Park Drive between Lynn
 Canyon Park picnic
 area and Ross Road
Sanitation River Dyke
 Road from Street
 Denis to Lynn Canyon
 Park
Hastings Creek Corridor
 Park between Allan
 Road and Hoskins
Trail between Williams
 and Chaucer
Lillooet Road—north of
 the Cemetery
Grouse Mountain Road
Anywhere on Baden-
Powell Trail
Pipe Line Road
Mosquito Creek Trail

Two women met on the
street and were updating
each other on the latest
news. One said, "Did you
hear that I got a Labrador
puppy for my husband?"
 The other replied, "Oh,
GOOD TRADE!"

Little Cates Park

Park at the tennis courts at Little Cates Park, and head down the trail marked "Dog Walk." There's a 7 a.m. group, an 8 a.m. group and a 9 a.m. group with at least a dozen dogs each. Go on through the main entrance to Cates Park. The trail continues on the other side and goes down towards the water. In the summer when the tide is out, head back along the beach, as you are not allowed in the main part of the park. You can get all the way back to the tennis courts this way. This is about a half-hour walk.

> — *Margy Gilmour, owner of Lucy, the Black Lab mutt*

Lynn Creek

There is a dirt road off Premier Street near Inter-river Park (which is along the bank of Lynn Creek). There's a brand new foot bridge, and the trails are great.

> — *Lori Staehling, owner of Golden Retrievers Ginger and Teddy*

Mosquito Creek

Mosquito Creek is great. Drive along Marine Drive to the intersection with Capilano Road and go north two blocks to the park. A sign says dogs aren't allowed, but there is a trail where you can take your dog. It follows the creek up under the highway, all the way to Queens. From there, you can turn around or go down a rougher trail on the other side of the creek. Or you can walk across Queens and pick up the trail again. It ends up at Skyline Drive. Also, there's an industrial area near Mosquito Creek Marina that is undeveloped and people walk their dogs in there. Go down Bewicke and cross the railroad track. Take the first right to the end of the road. This area is quiet and has a big open space.

> — *Haydee Mill, owner of Tika, a Border Collie X Blue Heeler*

Pitt Meadows

Pitt Meadows is surrounded by dikes. North of Lougheed Highway, on Harris Road, there is a big parking lot that gives you good access to the dikes. If you go one way it is nine miles (round trip), and the other way is six miles (round trip). Most of the dogs are well behaved and

under control. There's lots of wildlife: eagles, herons and ducks. It is nice and level, easy for biking or horse-back riding, too. My Dalmatian loves it.
— *Lesley Schreuder, owner of Tilly, a Dalmatian*

Port Moody
General Parks and Areas
Inlet, 3200 Block Murray Street
Old Orchard, 600 Block Bentley Road
Rocky Point, 2800 Block Murray Street
Shoreline Trail
Town Centre, 300 Ioco Road

Rocky Point Park
Enter from Rocky Point Park at the top of Burrard Inlet. If you follow the south side, you can walk around the head of the inlet and back. The trails are beautifully maintained and there is a walking trail as well as a separate biking/roller-blading/stroller path — everybody's happy. There is great bird watching: eagles, herons, kingfishers and lots of ducks. At the head of the inlet is a salmon enhancement project, the Noons Creek Hatchery, which is particularly interesting in the fall. In the summer, you can end your walk by treating yourself to Pa Joe's Fish and Chips at the park. Have a swim in a pool there too. There is an Italian ice cream stand as well!
— *Nancy Webber, owner of Keats, a Lougheed Highway Special*

Richmond
The City of Richmond Community Services Division publishes a great map and brochure called "Discover Richmond Trails." To obtain a brochure, call 276-4107. The Steveston trails connect Garry Point Park with the Steveston Historical Fishing Village, the Gulf of Georgia National Historic Site and the Britannia Heritage Shipyard.

East Richmond Trail
East Richmond Trail goes along River Road for 10 kilometres, from No. 6 Road to Boundary Road, and passes the No. 7 Road Pier, a woodlot and an old CN loading pier that has been restored for fishing and viewing.
— *"Discover Richmond Trails"*

The Top 4 Inappropriate (and Dangerous) Ways To Exercise a Dog
— British Columbia SPCA

• Exercising your dog while riding in a vehicle, either with a leash out the window or with the dog running off-leash in behind.

• Riding a bicycle with your dog on a leash.

• Skateboarding and leading a dog on leash.

• Roller-blading with your dog dragging behind you on a leash.

A man is talking with his butcher when a small dog trots in, holding some money in his mouth. The butcher says, "What'll it be today? Beef?" The little dog shakes his head. "How about chicken?" The dog shakes his head again. The butcher says, "Chops?" The dog wags his tail wildly. "Pork chops?" Dog shakes his head. "Lamb chops?" The tail wags frantically again. "Okay, lamb chops..." The butcher cuts the meat, takes the money from the dog's mouth, puts the wrapped chops in the dog's mouth, and the dog trots off.

"That was amazing!" says the man.

"Oh, he comes in every other day or so," says the butcher.

The man says, "I have to follow that dog and see

Garry Point Park

Garry Point Park is right by the Fraser River. There is lots of parking, and a bag dispenser if you forgot your bags. A nice trail runs along the water and passes a huge playing field. There is also a really beautiful view of the fishing boats and you can walk along the dikes for miles and miles. It is important to keep your dog under control, though, because there are bikes and horses.

— *Nilda Dorini, owner of Dalmatians Maax, Ella and Gina*

Iona Beach Regional Park

Dogs must be leashed. Even well-trained dogs can frighten or injure park wildlife and visitors. Please show courtesy to other park visitors by removing your dog's droppings. Dogs are not permitted in marsh areas.

— *Greater Vancouver Regional District*

Iona Beach is terrific. Located north of the airport, just past the sewage plant, it has tidal flats, marshes, grasslands, beaches and a four-kilometre trail on the Iona Jetty. You can walk or cycle out on the trail or walk on top of the huge deep-sea outfall pipe which carries the treated waste water to the tip of the jetty. The bird-watching is excellent, as is the plane- and boat-watching. You really do want to keep your dog leashed as the mud in the tidal flats is black, smelly and hard to remove.

— *Noel MacDonald, owner of Rosie the Border Collie*

Middle Arm Trail

The Middle Arm Trail is 5.5 kilometres long. A path along the dike stretches parallels to the roadway. There is a view of the airport, the City of Vancouver and the mountains. The trail also takes you to Dover Beach, where there is a viewing pier and seaplane landing area.

— *"Discover Richmond Trails"*

Richmond Interior Trails

Richmond Interior Trails lead to natural environments and wildliife habitats including the Richmond Nature Park, the CN Trial, the Bath Slough Trail, the Finn Road Trail and the Shell Road Trail.

— *"Discover Richmond Trails"*

Sea Island

Sea Island has cycling and driving routes that link together McDonald Beach Park and Iona Beach Regional Park.

— *"Discover Richmond Trails"*

South Dike Trail

The South Dike Trail follows the 6 kilometres along the South Arm of the Fraser River from the foot of No. 2 Road to the foot of Shell Road, passing by London's Landing, the London Farm/Gilbert Beach, a Sports Fishing Pier, Fin Slough and Horseshoe Slough.

— *"Discover Richmond Trails"*

West Dike Trail

The West Dike Trail is also 6 kilometres long. It looks out over tidal flats which extend 1.6 kilometres westward into the Georgia Strait and take you to Terra Nova, a park and observatory.

— *"Discover Richmond Trails"*

Surrey

Campbell Valley Regional Park

Dogs must be leashed. Two Dog Off-Leash Areas are currently being tested in the park along 4th Avenue and can be reserved for canine recreation events.

— *Greater Vancouver Regional District*

The nice part about the off-leash area in Campbell Valley Park is that you can let a dog that you trust take off and run. They can smell the flowers, let off some steam, do what they were naturally born to do. It is a beautiful park, with water areas, fields and forest.

— *Barbara Young, owner of Gordon Setters and English Pointers*

Dogwood Park

Located at 135th and 20th Avenue in South Surrey, Dogwood Park is especially for dogs and horses. There is a training area in which I rarely see horses, but often see dogs. There is a great pond for dog swimming, as well as trails and woods and a big, open play area. There is also a big notice board for dog events. People bring

where he lives!" He runs out, and spots the dog trotting up the block. He follows him until the dog runs up to a house, onto the porch, rises up on his hind legs, and rings the doorbell with his nose. A man comes to the door, takes the meat from the dog, then yells at him and locks him away in his crate.

The man watching is outraged. He storms up to the house and rings the doorbell. When the owner appears, the man says, "You know — that's the smartest dog I've ever seen. He goes to the butcher for you, *orders* the meat, *pays* for it, *brings* it home, *rings the damn doorbell*, and you treat him that way??"

"Yeah," says the man, "that's the third time this week he forgot his key!"

bags and put them on the provided hook. The regulars gather with their coffee to talk and watch their dogs play.
— *Carolyn Swayze, owner of Golden Retriever Grimsby*

Tynehead Regional Park
This park is located at the 168th Street and 102nd Avenue entrances to North Surrey. At the 168th Street entrance is an off-leash area which may be reserved for recreation events. Dogs must always be under owner's control. In the rest of the park, dogs must be on a leash and aren't allowed in the Serpentine River. Please pick up after your dog.
— *Greater Vancouver Regional District*

Vancouver
Parks Around Town
We like the Stanley Park seawall because it is a good place for Sancho to practice his obedience by heeling closely. For more of a wander we go to Queen Elizabeth Park, and for a fun play session we join the gang at Vanier Park on weekend mornings. And, for our close-to-home morning and after-work doggie group meetings, we go to Hillcrest Park, near Nat Bailey Stadium.
—*Laureen Miki, owner of Sancho the Portuguese Water Dog.*

Fraser River Park
Fraser River Park at 75th and Angus is the right length of walk for my older dogs. We can do the circuit in about a half hour. At low tide you can walk on the beach. Ninety percent of the people we see there have dogs. A bus of disabled adults shows up very often and they love the dogs. People are responsible dog owners — there is little in the way of dog feces on the trails. It's a good park because there are a lot of people around, it is safe for seniors, and there is good bird watching too.
— *Maureen Meikle, owner of Jessie, Golden Setter X, and Meg the Westie*

Jericho
My favourite thing to do is to walk on wonderful Jericho Beach when the ticket people are still sleeping.
— *Martine, owner of Othello the Giant Schnauzer*

Q: Why do dogs follow their owners?

A: It's the path of leash resistance.

Pacific Spirit Regional Park, UBC Endowment Lands
Located at SW Marine Drive to NW Marine Drive
between Camosun Street and Acadia Road, this park
contains 763 hectares of forest and foreshore separating
the city from the University of BC. Dogs must be under
control at all times. For health reasons and to protect
sensitive environments, dogs may be prohibited from
sections of the park. Watch for signs. Please clean up
after your dog.
— *Greater Vancouver Regional District*

I have a two-year-old daughter and a five-year-old Golden
Retriever guide dog. My wife and I enjoy the natural
features of Pacific Spirit Park. Why should we have our
peace of mind stressed out because of the selfish
behaviour of the me-first mountain bikers? There are a
lot of them who fail to yield right of way, they don't
provide courtesy calls when passing from behind and
there is a blatant contravention of what are marked as
"no biking" areas. They have snatched the signs and
ruined the flora and fauna and made it tough for us to
have a quiet walk. Those of us with families enjoy this
park because of its high level of access, which is ironic
because that has become part of the problem. We want
to preserve this natural area for our kids. We are going
to have to learn to get along before injuries and
subsequent interventions force us to take action.
— *Bruce Gilmour, owner of Solomon, the Golden
Retriever*

Southlands
Southlands, a.k.a. "The Flats," is a pocket of the city
directly south of Kerrisdale. It is bordered on the north
by S.W. Marine Drive and 49th Avenue, on the south by
the Fraser River, on the east by the McCleery Public Golf
Course and on the west by the Point Grey Golf Club. It
covers about 90 acres. It is flat. And right at the water
line it is wet — witness the enormous weeping willow
trees. Southlands is an odd but charming mishmash, from
enormous new mansions to funny old rundown houses
with dilapidated barns, and a small number of businesses,
mostly nurseries. The zoning is for semi-rural and
equestrian use, and limited agriculture. Dogs love the

For more walks than your
two feet, and your dog's
four, can imagine, see:
*109 Walks in British
Columbia's Lower
Mainland,* by Mary and
David Macaree (Douglas
and McIntyre);
*Nature Walks around
Vancouver,* by Jean Cousins
(Greystone Books);
Day Trips from Vancouver,
by Jack Christie (Greystone
Books).

smells here, and as it is so small, it makes for a good walkabout. Along the Fraser River, on the south edge, is a great trail with boats galore to watch. It is across from Iona Island, the airport and a boat-launching area. There is a path between the water and the Point Grey Golf Course which will take you up to S.W. Marine Drive, where a pedestrian crossing will get you over to Pacific Spirit Regional Park. Watch for horses.

— *Marg and Noel, and Rosie the Border Collie*

West Vancouver

The following list of areas where dogs are prohibited and permitted in this area is reprinted from the Corporation of the District of West Vancouver's excellent brochure, "Dog Regulations."

A. Areas where Dogs are Prohibited:

All playgrounds, playing
   fields, beaches,
   fitness circuits,
   running tracks, golf
   courses, tennis courts
   and bowling greens
Centennial Seawalks,
   all floats, piers and
   public buildings in
   parks
John Lawson Park
Dundarave Park
Klahanie Park
Hugo Ray Park
Memorial Park
Whytecliff Park, west
   of Marine Drive
Recreation Centre site
Benbow Park
Horseshoe Bay Park
Irwin Park
Klee Wyck Park
Parc Verdun
Glenmore Park
Tantalus Park

West Bay Park
Balmy Beach
   (Parthenon)
Capilano View
   Cemetery
Ambleside Park
Ambleside Landing
   (foot of 14th)

B. Areas Where Dogs are Permitted on Leash:

Leyland Park
Hay Park
Chatwin Park
John Richardsson Park
Klootchman Park
Hidhurst Park
Trail Park
Charwell Park
Westridge Park (except
   tennis court and
   playground)
Caulfeild Park (except
   beach)
Crosscreek Park
Ambleside Park

Annual Dog Walks

Canadian Guide Dogs for the Blind Walk
The last Sunday in May at Brockton Oval.

SPCA Walk-a-Thon (Bark in the Park)
The second Sunday in September at Brockton Oval.

Dogathon
Walk with your dogs and pledge to the Variety Club. Usually the last Saturday of April. An event to raise money for children that are physically and/or mentally challenged. North Vancouver and in White Rock at Dogwood Park. Contact the Variety Club.

Bassett Hound Walk
The first Sunday in May, rain or shine. This was the original Vancouver dog walk.

C. Areas Where Dogs are Permitted Fully Controlled by Owners but not on Leash:

Hollyburn Ridge (dogs should not be permitted to interfere with skiers, or to molest deer and other wildlife in the area)

Ambleside Park, extreme easterly portion from Fitness Circuit parking lot east

Douglas Woodward Park

McKechnie Park (except tennis courts)

Lighthouse Park

Seaview Walk (Gleneagles Area)

Ballantree Park (except playground and Fitness Circuit)

Cypress Falls Park (except developed southwest portion)

Piccadilly Park

Whytecliff Park, east portion

Centennial Seawall (from 19th on Marine Drive ONLY to 24th), north of fence

Centennial Seawall

Walking your dog on the Centennial Seawall takes a small leap of faith. When I first took my dog there, I didn't know if she would go up to the train tracks. If you don't know exactly what your dog is going to do, it makes for a tense walk. Also, there are gaps in the fence every few hundred metres, and of course your dog wants to join you. It also makes for the occasional stand-off: Dogs end up nose-to-nose and they don't know quite what to do. If you are walking for your dog and not for you, go to the Ambleside Dog Park instead.

    — Hugh Wilson, owner of Scout, the Golden Retriever

White Rock
Centennial Park

(16th Avenue and 14600 block)

This park used to be called Mann Park — Mrs. Mann gave it to the city. They changed the name in 1967. There is a jogging trail through a lovely forested area which is cool in the summer. There is a stream going to the beach. And there are stairs to take you down to the beach as well.

    — Elaine Bergen, owner of Alvie, the tan-and-white Cocker Spaniel

A lady awoke one morning and discovered her dog was not moving. She called her vet, who asked her to bring the dog in. After a brief examination, the vet pronounced the dog dead.

"Are you sure?" the distraught woman asked. "He was a great family pet. Isn't there anything else you can do?" The vet paused for a moment and said, "There is one more thing we can do." He left the room for a moment and came back carrying a large cage with a cat in it. The vet opened the cage door and the cat walked over to the dog. The cat sniffed the dog from head to toe and walked back to the cage.

"Well, that confirms it," the vet announced. "Your dog is dead." Satisfied that the vet had done everything he possibly could, the woman sighed, "How much do I owe you?"

"That will be $330," the vet replied.

"I don't believe it!" screamed the woman. "What did you do that cost $330??"

"Well," the vet replied, "it's $30 for the office visit and $300 for the cat scan.

Semiahmoo Park

At East Beach in Semiahmoo Park (160th and Marine Drive — the furthest beach to the south), the Little Campbell flows out to Semhiamoo Bay. Folks let dogs off leash there to swim.

> — *Carolyn Swayze, owner of Grimsby the Golden Retriever*

Volkssporting

Volkssporting translates as "sports for the ordinary people." In the Lower Mainland, there are four Volkssporting clubs that focus on non-competitive walking. The minimum walking distance is 10 kilometres and the maximum is marathon distance (42 kilometres). Each club has a schedule of walks all over the Lower Mainland and throughout the province (and even into other countries!). Many of the organized walks are appropriate for dogs, so call the contact person ahead of time to check.

Richmond Trailblazers Volkssport Club
Manfred Koestlmaier
274-3259

Surrey Trekkers Volkssport Club
Cheryl Hildebrand
943-8504

Vancouver 'Venturers Volkssport Club
Verni Brown
682-8390

Westcoast Walkers Volkssport Club (Coquitlam)
Eleanor Paugh
552-1132

Q: What's worse than raining cats and dogs?

A: Hailing taxis!

PROFESSIONAL DOG WALKERS

Walking When You Can't

What a concept: coming home to a happy and well-exercised dog. Dog walkers pick up dogs from the owners' homes and return the dogs after walking them. Rates vary from $8 to $13 per pick-up. Discounts are often given for more than one dog, or more than one pick-up, per walk. Some of these same companies will also do pet sitting in your home.

Aldergrove
TLC In Home Pet Sitters
856-4866
Pick-up and delivery dog walking.

Burnaby
The Purple Leash
Jennifer Lloyd
230-5514

Coquitlam
Luv-A-Pet
464-CARE (2273)

Langley
TLC In Home Pet Sitters
856-4866
Pick-up and delivery dog walking.

New Westminster
Tiffany's Doggy Salon
526-5026

North Vancouver
Adrienne Wood
983-3994

Dogs and Company
Michelle Nozeres
649-4387 (cell) or 986-1309

Dog Around the Block

Dog around the block,
  sniff,
Hydrant sniffing, corner,
  grating,
Sniffing, always, starting
  forward,
Backward, dragging,
  sniffing backward,
Leash at taut, leash at
  dangle,
Leash in people's feet
  entangle—
Sniffing dog, apprised of
  smellings,
Love of life, and fronts of
  dwellings,
Meeting enemies,
Loving old acquaintance,
  sniff,
Sniffing hydrant for
  reminders,
Leg against the wall, raise,
Leaving grating, corner
  greeting,
Chance for meeting, sniff,
  meeting,
Meeting, telling, news of
  smelling,
Nose to tail, tail to nose,
Rigid, careful, pose,
Liking, partly liking, hating,
Then another hydrant,
  grating,
Leash at taut, leash at
  dangle,
Tangle, sniff, untangle,
Dog around the block,
  sniff.
— E.B. White

One day, a sign appeared in an office window. It read: "Help wanted. Must type 70 words a minute. Must be computer literate. Must be bilingual. An equal opportunity employer." A dog ambling down the street saw the sign, walked in, and applied for the job.

The office manager said, "I can't hire a dog for this job." The dog pointed to the line: "An equal opportunity employer." So the manager said, "Okay, take this letter and type it." The dog went off to the word processor and returned a minute later with the finished letter, perfectly formatted. The manager said: "Here's a problem. Write a computer program for it and run it." Fifteen minutes later, the dog came back with the correct answer. The manager still wasn't convinced. "I can't hire a dog for this position," he said. "You've got to be bilingual."

The dog looked up at the manager and said, "Meow."

Happy Pet Sitters
Sylvia
984-9477

The Laughing Dog Pet Care Services
Jo-Anne or Helene
987-8057

Peace of Mind Pet Services
Julie Bryson
984-7395
Dog walking, pet ambulance and geriatric care.

The Pet Set In-Home Pet Sitting
Frances Bates
926-9821

The Pet Sitters
Teri Booth
980-0438

The Purple Leash
Jennifer Lloyd
230-5514

Rest Assured, Your Home Sentry and Pet Care Service
Carol Hurrell
984-2822

Richmond
House Minders
Jan McIntyre
272-4731

Perfect Pet Care
Deborah Wolfe
878-0364

Surrey
Rosie's Pet Services
589-4314 or 435-6160

TLC In Home Pet Sitters
Pick-up and delivery dog walking.
856-4866

Vancouver
I Love Dogs
Sue Laidlaw and Dawn McDonald
228-1945 or 631-0300

Collie Flower Animal Service
Heather Culliford
325-5810

Grizzly's Dog Walking
Colleen Sheridan
738-2847

Kidd Kare Pet Services
329-3736
Pet taxi all over Greater Vancouver; also does day care, kennel-free boarding, pick-up and delivery dogwalking. Walks to beach and parks.

Launderdog
685-2306
Dogwalking and daycare, full-serve and self-serve washing, some pet-supplies.

Paws at Home
Nicole
739-1818
Dog walking, pet sitting.

o.k, O.k, i admit ....
the neighbour's
cat was tasty.

Perfect Pet Care
Deborah Wolfe
878-0364
Pet sitting, training, walking.

The Pet Nanny
Nicole LeBlanc
899-431
Dog walking, pet sitting, pet taxi.

Petsitting
Sandy Morris
601-0595

Heather Culliford, on the professional dog walker's credo: "Always carry more poop bags than you think you'll need."

Point Grey Veterenary Clinic
228-1714
Walking, grooming, full veterinary service, shop, training (semi- and private lessons), boarding, day care.

TLC Professional Dog Exerciser
Andrew Fawcett
224-0897

Tuskayla Dog Walking Services
Louise or Nicola
263-6167

Whiskers Pet Services
551-5041
West Side and West End, walks in Pacific Spirit Park, pet sitting.

West Vancouver
The North Shore Paw Prince
Adrienne
983-3994

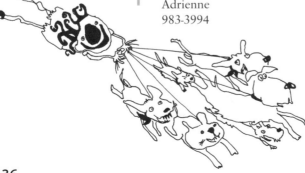

A DOG WALKER'S TALE

We're Hunting Wabbits

— *Bill Richardson*

When I die, and some tombstone carver is charged with the odious task of inscribing my final summation in marble, he or she will not have to fret over the intricacies of chiseling the word "athletic." It is not an adjective that has ever been used in conjunction with my name. From earliest childhood, my relationship with the hurly-burly world of game playing has been simple and uncluttered. We don't like each other. We don't get along. There is no reason to suspect that this might ever change.

There is only one sport I have become involved with of late, albeit in an ancillary capacity, and that is hunting. First, though, let me make one thing clear. I have always thought that hunting was rebarbative when undertaken principally with sport in mind, rather than for reasons of simple survival. Human inventiveness is not praiseworthy when it is turned to using weapons against some creature armed only with its intangible wits — particularly when the object of the exercise is to cull some part of its physical being to mount on a plaque and decorate a wall. I can think of few spectacles more sick-making than the sight of a yahoo-piloted 4x4 van, decorated with a deer carcass, idling at a red light at the corner of Vancouver's Georgia and Bute. Nonetheless, my association with my dog Smoke, a terrier, has made me accessory to a number of hunting excursions.

Smoke is placid, quiet, self-contained, gentle, loyal,

Photograph of Smoke by Heather Culliford

Q: What kind of dog lives in the forest?

A: A dogwood.

slow moving and barrel-shaped. She is good with children. Old people adore her. People stop to pet her in the middle of busy intersections. Everything about her broadcasts "benign." But given half a chance, and the right game, she turns into a killing machine that is frightening to behold.

The first sign of Smoke's deadly gift came on the day she emerged from the kitchen with a tail hanging out of her mouth — a tail that was not her own. Imagine my amazement! In the first place, I had no notion whatsoever that I was sharing my apartment with *Rodentia*. I was surprised that this vacant, innocuous dog had the savvy to catch anything more dramatic than a cold. And I was very surprised to see the reverential way she treated her prey. She lavished the kind of attention on it she'd never accorded her outlandishly priced rubber doggy toys. She gave it the careful deliberation a child gives to a lollipop, sucking it slowly, turning it over and over in her mouth, milking it for every last bit of flavor. Then she spat it out, curled up on the couch and drifted into a satisfied sleep. Some minutes passed before I could bring myself to examine the carcass. There was little to indicate that it had only a few minutes before been a living thing. It was about the size and shape and texture of the buttons on my mother's muskrat coat.

Smoke's previously unheralded skills as a furry Diana were a boon over the next few weeks. The first mouse was a harbinger of a plague of Old Testament proportions. As Smoke's activities intensified, there were no tender-hearted sympathizers to call down calumnies on her head or on mine. Smoke seemed to suffer no ill effects from the ingestion of fresh meat. The only drawback was that she would come to bed with mouse on her.

I was not so sanguine when she went public at Jericho Beach. This is an area much favoured by dog walkers. In the last few years, it has also become home to an increasingly populous colony of rabbits. There is a whole squad of well-meaning but half-mad people who look out for the welfare of these lapin invaders. They create little lodges for them, ply them with carrots and lettuce, and through this charity strip them of the wariness in which rabbits ought properly to be steeped. I had no idea how placid and slow they had become until the day Smoke emerged from amongst the brambles with a squirming, dove-grey bunny in her jaws. One shake of her terrier head and it was a done deal.

Smoke is a dog of many fine qualities, but discretion is not among them. She had the bad sense to off the poor creature in front of one of the self-appointed guardians of haredom, an English woman with tightly permed white hair and snapping eyes. I don't suppose she was personally acquainted with the rabbit, but she ranted and carried on as though she had just come upon one of Herod's soldiers wiping the blood from his sword. Smoke set down her burden and rolled in it, which didn't help matters. There was nothing I could say to satisfy the woman, and nothing I could do to effect a resurrection, and eventually she stalked away, muttering words like "irresponsible," which is exactly the adjective I apply to people who encourage rabbits to believe they live in a world where no harm can befall them.

I picked up the corpse. The warmth that was a by-product of living was leaving it. There was no blood, no sign of a struggle. I felt neither pity nor exultation. Rather, I felt something I can only describe as privilege at having witnessed this transaction between two animals who could never have ascribed such qualities as guilt or anger to the acting out of their business. It had been a beautiful little thing. It still was. For just a moment, I caught a glimmer of something I hope hunters feel in the quiet moment when they stand over the animal they've dispatched. Holiness, really. Wonder, at all that was there and no longer is.

Then, as there was nothing else to be done, I threw the lapsed rabbit as far into the blackberry brambles as I could, leashed the triumphant Smoke and headed back to the car. She sat in the back seat and beamed out at the passing traffic. Other drivers smiled. Children waved. None of them could guess that this beguiling canine Miss Daisy was an assassin of the first water. None of them could guess what had just transpired on the grassy knoll we were leaving behind.

Q: What dog has ticks?

A: A watch dog.

139

Portrait by
Judy Fry

Portrait by
Wendy Grossman

V. Dog Training, Competitions & Sports

There is nothing like a well trained dog. Most of us view training as a lifetime commitment — we have learned the hard way that you have to keep at it and that dogs need to be constantly challenged and disciplined. So far, our Border Collie Rosie has had three different experiences with trainers. As Marion Postgate, a well-respected trainer in the Lower Mainland, suggests in this chapter: you've got to shop around. Marion has graciously put together some guidelines for choosing a training class. Much information can be gleaned from books as well, and Dr. Stanley Coren, a trainer for many years with the Vancouver Dog Obedience Club, has shared some of his favourites with us.

There are many levels of training, of course, and some are competitive. In this chapter I have attempted to unravel some of the intricacies of the dog competition world, including Obedience and Conformation. If competing in these categories isn't your thing, perhaps the fast-growing world of dog sports is. Even if you and your dog don't want to play, at least go watch some of these sports — from agility to musical freestyle to field trials to weight-pulling, they are a hoot! Almost every breed of dog — including mixed-breed dogs — can get involved in some of the sports included here. Dog sports are some of the best ways to combine training and playing. They are fun for the owner, the dog — and the spectator, too!

TRAINING YOUR DOG

The Benefits of a Trained Dog

— *FIDO*

It sits when told to do so.
It leaves guests alone when they are eating.
It will not jump up on guests.
It will not take over the house.
It knows you're the boss.
It comes when called and does not stray.
It does not strain on the leash and walk YOU.
It is not a nuisance to your neighbours.
It chews only on items that are its toys.
It does not bark endlessly.
It will not chase other dogs or cats.
It loves you for telling it what you want because it really
    wants you to be happy.

Choosing a Training Class

— *Marion Postgate, trainer and obedience judge*

Before going to a training class, teach your puppy or dog manners at home. Get a good book or videotape on training, and start. Seek out a "puppy kindergarten" for puppies three to five months of age, one that teaches some basic training, not just a puppy play session. (Puppies and dogs socialize and bond very readily with other dogs, and learn to ignore their human pack. Beware of the gangs playing in the park.)

If you are inexperienced, or not confident about how to manage a new pet, you might hire a private trainer for one-on-one advice and instruction at home. Or you may prefer a professional to do the actual training, on a daily basis, at your home or at a kennel. In any case, a trainer will ask you to commit to continuing the training the dog has received — and the bond created between you and your dog is worth it.

Once you have done some home training, join a class. Even professional trainers do this. A class situation enables you to polish your dog's lessons in a situation that is very distracting — the presence of other dogs — and allows both you and your dog to do a little controlled socializing. Consider the following factors in choosing a class:

The instructor: Success depends upon the effectiveness of the teaching. Seek recommendations from your dog's breeder or veterinarian, or other owners whose dogs appear well trained. There are no standards in Canada for accrediting dog trainers. Find out how much experience a trainer has, and in what areas of dog training. One of the best recommendations is that a trainer has competed regularly in CKC Obedience Trials, achieving utility titles on several dogs, ideally of different breeds. Other trainers may have years of good experience in behavioural problems and basic training. All should have an obvious rapport with dogs and an ability to communicate with owners. A sense of humour also helps!

Location: For convenience, most owners prefer a class close to home. In Vancouver, you may not find one. A city the size of Vancouver *should* support five or six active Obedience Training Clubs, which could offer many levels of training and social activity for students and members. Unfortunately, because of the cost and lack of facilities, only one such club exists. Classes offered through community centres and night school are the alternative, but rarely offer training beyond an elementary level. Most are held indoors in gyms or activity rooms; a few are held outdoors. As a rule, classes are inexpensive but large. Instruction is aimed at basic training for the average dog. Owners wanting higher levels of training will have to travel to the Fraser Valley to private training centres.

Classes: Classes are usually offered in eight to 12 week modules for one hour a week, including Puppy Kindergarten and Beginners. If you switch from one instructor to another at higher levels, check that you enroll in a class suited to you and your dog's accomplishments. Advanced classes might mean off-leash work on basics, or search and rescue scent work.

Finally, expect to do homework. Dogs need at least 40 hours of formal training for basic control, and more for reliable off-leash control such as coming or dropping at a distance in the presence of any distraction. Practicing 20 minutes a day, Sundays off, plus informal training for

Q: What is a female dog's favourite perfume?

A: Kennel No. 5.

two sets of eight-week classes, is only 32 hours. An additional year of regular practice will result in a beautifully trained dog for many years to come.

Obedience Clubs

North Vancouver
Capilano Obedience Club
Barbara Merkley
921-7834
Offers beginners and advanced obedience and/or obedience trials.

Richmond
Richmond Dog Fanciers Association
Lil Geddes
241-0705
A non-profit organization that promotes responsible dog ownership. Meets four nights a week for obedience classes, one night for confirmation showing and one night for junior handling. Also organizes regular dog walks and a two-day trial in June.

Vancouver
Vancouver Dog Obedience Club
Dr. Stanley Coren
822-6458
Non-profit club started 40 years ago by Mrs. Jean Lyle. Follows Blanche Saunders' training methods. Meets two evenings a week. Classes limited to 15. Supports SPCA, FIDO and Wildlife Rescue.

Trainers & Behaviourists

These trainers are listed alphabetically by name, but not by location — many of these trainers will travel to different locations within the Lower Mainland.

Aldergrove Kennels
26306 56th Ave.
856-DOGS, Fax: 856-5554, ext. 5025
Certified dog trainer, specializing in training family pets.

Behaviour problems are the biggest reasons people surrender dogs to shelters, and biting is the Number One problem.

144

A+ Dog Obedience
1001-4900 Francis Rd.
Richmond
272-3040
e-mail: floss100@aol.com
Registered Animal Health Technician and certified trainer. Problem prevention and behaviour modification. Puppy groups and small obedience classes.

Abuse Free Dog Training
23697 Lougheed Hwy.
Maple Ridge
467-0494
Specialize in in-home obedience training, behaviour problem solving and aggression de-programming.

Academy of Dog Training
2920 Carolina St.
Vancouver
873-3660
In-kennel training in Abbotsford. Confidence-oriented protection work. Abuse-free training. Government registered trade school for dog trainers.

Alabon Country Kennels
20391 Westminster Hwy.
Richmond
270-2822
Basic obedience training.

Animal Profiles
648 Moody Ave.
North Vancouver
988-4642
Animal behaviour consultant, videotape analysis, personalized dog training.

Amore Pet Services
8250 Cartier St.
Vancouver
263-4963
Holistic approach to communicating, feeding and understanding your dog.

"The ultimate personal protection dog is an outgoing working dog that is friendly, socializes well with others and is trustworthy. Guard dogs are trained with pain and fear-motivated aggression. It isn't easy for them to switch handlers, and they are not dogs for the city. In particular, they are not to be trusted off-leash."
— Paul Vertanen,
Academy of Dog Training

Best Behavior Dog Training
773-0012 or 631-0300
Obedience-puppy training, behavioural problem solving, walking, sitting. Certified, specializing in positive and motivational techniques.

Birkland Kennels
23779 32nd Ave.
Langley
530-0077
Obedience, tracking, protection.

Q: When will a puppy go with you to the movies?

A: When you promise to buy it pup-corn.

Donna Bradley
857-0490
Specializes in competitive obedience training. One-on-one or small classes. Has a training facility in Aldergrove.

Brunton Canine Training Services
1310 Monashee Dr.
North Vancouver
988-6775
website: http://www.thenerve2.com/silk/brunton
Family training and professional dog trainer courses. Home of the Companion Concept Programme. Brunton's training video *Dog Obedience Training...the Easy Way* is in most public libraries. Distance learning available soon.

Brynjulf Canine Services
9436 184th St.
Surrey
882-3946
Specializes in obedience competitions. Boarding Kennels, training, grooming and breeding of Dobermans and German Pinschers.

Camp Critters
18030-32nd Ave.
Surrey
541-4138

Canadian Institute Of Professional Dog Training
Tony Parker
19564 16 Ave.
Surrey
538-5529
Private Post Secondary Institution. Spin-off from British Institute of Police Dog Trainers. Registered and bonded. Also holds a registry of qualified trainers.

Canine Caretakers
Evelyn Bliss
270-0309
Agility, flyball, obedience, conformation handling, behavioural counseling and herbal consulting.

Canine Connection
22346 Loughheed Hwy.
Maple Ridge
463-7422
Kindergarten, puppy, intermediate and advanced obedience, show-obedience, evening group classes.

Cinemazoo Animal Agency Ltd
6939 Hastings St.
Burnaby
299-6963
Trains all kinds of animals.

Countryside Kennels
558 Prairie Ave.
Coquitlam
945-0125
Basic on-leash training: sit, come, stay, down etc. Behaviour problems addressed. Also offer grooming, daycare, boarding.

Custom Canine
Burnaby
451-1293
Kathy and Gary Gibson, Behaviourists. Building healthy relationships with your dog. One-on-one problem solving classes. Concentrate on developing the dog's skills and abilities to be self-controlled, reliable, contributing

"The cat will mew and dog will have his day."
— William Shakespeare,
Hamlet

members of a household. Soon to open a training centre, based on Canine Connections, the program at the Burnaby Correctional Centre for Women which operated from 1989 to 1996. Its goal is developing character and personality of dogs and people. Children's program too.

Genevieve Dawson
Surrey
581-3461
Basic obedience training, one-on-one.

Dog Gone Good Training Inc.
Delores Wall
1284 - 242nd St.
Langley
533-8066
website: http://www.compupets.com/doggone.html#top
Certified. Supportive training for the family dog and behaviour consultation services. Non-abusive, with positive and motivational reinforcement. Private sessions in your home or at our training facility in Langley; group sessions offered in Vancouver and White Rock. Canine Good Citizen courses offered through the Vancouver School Board and other locations. Head volunteer trainer, Vancouver SPCA. Offer Sunday morning puppy and beginner classes.

Note: SPCA Volunteer Dog Walkers must go through an orientation meeting and a handling class before they can take out dogs. For information, call Rita Britton, volunteer coordinator, at 301-1642.

Marilyn Ewing Obedience Training
Delta
940-0367

Garry Galt
Coquitlam
464-9133
Teaches group lessons at various community centres, and gives private lessons from puppy to behavioural and aggression challenges.

Hollywood North Canine Training and Talent Agency
104 - 1037 W. Broadway
Vancouver
738-1568
CD, CDX and UD (CKC's Obedience), Musical
Freestyle, herding, personal protection dogs and Canine
Good Citizen course at three levels.

Denise Holowolenko
221-PUPS (7877)
Thirty years teaching family (not competition) obedience
from a common sense perspective, accentuating the
positive. Member Association of Pet Dog Trainers
(APDT).

Human Dog Leadership Inc.
818 Miller Ave.
Coquitlam
939-0803
Training people to communicate with dogs in Dog
Language and train them Nature's way. Administer
Canine Good Citizens test.

Ann W. Jackson
922-3851
Behaviorist and motivational trainer on the North Shore
(including Squamish and Lions Bay). All courses include
emergency first aid, preventive health care, a lecture night
on dog psychology, development during the dog's first
year and problem-solving hints.

Klahanie Kennels
18718 - 32nd Ave.
Vancouver
541-2772
Boarding. Obedience and behaviour modification.

Paddy McGurin
(250) 226-7712
Lives in Nelson but comes to Vancouver monthly for one-
on-one training. Motto: "I want you to have a dog you
can take anywhere!"
e-mail: paddy@netidea

The Young Puppy
There was a young puppy
 called Howard,
Who at fighting was rather
 a coward;
He never quite ran
 when the battle began,
But he started at once to
 bow-wow hard.
— A.A. Milne

149

Q: What do you call a
puppy sleeping on his
blanket?

A: A hot dog.

Meadow View Acres
Bonnie/Moe Ritch
4044 - 184th St.
Surrey
574-2323
Training, boarding, grooming.

Mutts 'n Manners
Rita Britton, coordinator
1205 E. 7th St.
Vancouver
301-1642
Vancouver SPCA Sunday morning dog obedience classes.

North American Guard Dog & Kenneling Services Ltd.
16238 - 56th St.
Surrey
574-9757
Behaviour modification, training of dog trainers. Kennels, grooming.

Northwest Dog Training Academy
Dennis Brunton
1310 Monashee St.
North Vancouver
985-4913
One of the largest boarding and training facilities in BC. Offer obedience, protection, tracking and other specialty training.

Obedience Plus
Chief Trainer: Werner Harder
3387 Kingsway
Vancouver
435-5505

100% Pet Care
Leanne
203 E. 6th Ave.
Vancouver
879-0077
Training and problems.

One on One Basic Obedience
15017 - 108th Ave.
Surrey: 581-346

Perfect Pet Care
Deborah Wolfe
878-0364
Author of *Good Dog! Positive Training Techniques*. Does behaviour and trick training.

Marion Postgate
263-9082
Trainer since 1953. Teaches for VSB night school, North Shore Neighbourhood House and Junior Kennel Club (see "Kids & Dogs," page 217). Obedience judge and CKC obedience representative.

Todd Redmond
1843 Chesterfield Ave.
North Vancouver
980-0786

Train 'n' Show
Muriel Bereziak
936-9191
Teaches puppy and adult classes in Guildford at the Anglican Church of the Epiphany on Tuesdays. Obedience classes, too.

Richmond Kennels
1350 Blundell Rd.
Richmond
273-6553
Trainer: Tammy Routley, speaks Japanese.

Rondivills
16640 Westminster Hwy.
Richmond
278-7181
Training, boarding, grooming.

Q: Where do you put your dog if you don't want its barking to bother people?

A: In a barking lot.

Setter Straight Mobile Dog Trainer
463-7578
Obedience classes.

Kim Solberg
11463 - 205th St.
Maple Ridge
465-6592 / 640-0132 (pager)
Basic obedience, positive motivational methods, behavioural problem-solving. President of Rottweiler Club. Does all-breed obedience training, tracking, German-style show-obedience.

Surrey Dog Obedience Training
Gary/Shirley Roe
16508 - 60 Ave.
Surrey
574-5937
The club trains for obedience (puppy kindergarten to more advanced work) and tracking in Cloverdale and South Surrey. Puts on Canadian Kennel Club Tracking Trials. Addresses in-home dog behavioural problems in Surrey, Delta, Langley and White Rock.

TK Canine Training Centre
7850 River Rd.
Richmond
Pager: 443-4989
Don Chan, K9 Master Trainer, speaks Cantonese.
Basic obedience, advanced and specialist dog training.

TNT Obedience Training
Janice Gunn
27624 Watson Rd.
Aldergrove
857-9891
Obedience, group and private lessons. Specializing in competition training and problem solving. Also puppy classes for dogs from 12 weeks to eight months old. Classes held in the Aldergrove training building.

Total Recall Dog Obedience
Lisa Frederick
543-0135
Obedience classes (private, or small class sizes), motivational methods. In-house boarding and training.

Underwood's Dog Obedience
Ray Underwood
534-7404
Classes and private lessons in competitive and basic obedience.

Westcoast Canine Services
Jill Kirkpatrick
13380 - 96th Ave.
Surrey
588-1317; 588-1317
Private and group non-abusive training. Specialize in help with behavioural problems. Booklet available.

Willchris Kennels Ltd.
14824 - 40th. Ave.
Surrey
576-9603
Obedience, kennels, daycare.

Associations

Association of Canine Behavioural Consultants
Gary Gibson, Executive Director
243 - 4609 Kingsway
Burnaby
451-1293
Promote and provide humane education about the human/canine relationship.

Canadian Association of Professional Pet Dog Trainers
177 Ronan Ave.
Toronto, Ontario
M4N 2Y5
(416) 789-0767

When Byron's favourite dog died, the poet had a marble monument erected to his memory, with this inscription:
Near this spot are deposited the Remains of one Who possessed Beauty without Vanity, Strength without Insolence, Courage without Ferocity, and all the Virtues of Man without his Vices.
This Praise, which would be unmeaning flattery if inscribed over Human Ashes, is but a just tribute to the Memory of Boatswain, a Dog, who was born at Newfoundland, May 1803, and died at Newstead Abbey, November 18, 1808.

Dr. Stanley Coren's Favourite Training Books

— Dr. Stanley Coren

1. *The Invisible Leash: A Better Way to Communicate With Your Dog*, by Myrna M. Milani (Signet Books).
This is an inexpensive little paperback that addresses the basics of civilizing your dog as a companion. It has a simple and helpful philosophy for dealing with dogs and is a great introduction for people who have never had a dog before.

2. *Mother Knows Best: The Natural Way to Train Your Dog*, by Carol Lea Benjamin (Howell Books).
Anything by Benjamin is both readable and useful. Her drawings will make you smile. This is a very basic book for beginning training of your dog.

3. *The Complete Idiot's Guide to Choosing, Training and Raising a Dog*, by Sarah Hodgson (Alpha Books).
Hodgson has put out a number of books recently. All have the same sound information on basic training . I like this one is a bit better than the others because of the information on dog selection that it includes.

4. *The Complete Dog Training Manual*, by Bruce Fogle (RD Press).
Fogle writes splendid books about dogs. Recently he has switched to producing books that are richly illustrated, where the pictures carry much of the information. This is the case for this volume, which contains lots of basic dog training and useful information on playing with your dog and solving simple problems.

5. *Natural Dog Training*, by Kevin Behan (Morrow).
The approach used in this book is different from most of the others. It covers the information needed for teaching your dog basic commands, and includes sections on what to do with difficult dogs.

6. *How To Be Your Dog's Best Friend*, by Job Michael Evans (with the Monks of New Skete) (Little, Brown & Company).

This book is a "must have" for everyone who wants to train and understand dogs. It is a good read as well as being informative. Evans' other books are oriented toward curing problem behaviors and they are all worth a look if your dog is driving you crazy with some of the things that it is doing.

7. *Playtraining Your Dog*, by Patricia Gail Burnham (St. Martin's Press).
This is one of the best books available for people who want to train their dogs for obedience competition. The idea of playtraining is novel. How well it works is shown by the fact that Burnham trains Greyhounds for obedience work, and this is not a breed that is well known for trainability.

8. *Beyond Basic Dog Training*, by Diane L. Bauman (Howell Books).
This is one of the standard, reliable books on training a dog for higher levels of obedience competition. Bauman has a good feeling for dogs and presents her material in a clear workable manner that is easy to follow.

9. *Don't Shoot the Dog: The New Art of Teaching and Training*, by Karen Pryor (Bantam Books).
This is a book on the philosophy and science of training, rather than on teaching basic commands. Specifically, it shows you how to use rewards to shape your dog's behavior. After you train the dog using these ideas, you can go on to use the same principles to train your kids.

10. *Dog Tricks: Teaching Your Dog to be Useful, Fun and Entertaining*, by Capt. Arthur J. Haggerty and Carol Lea Benjamin (Howell Books).
This book is just for fun, but some of the tricks are useful as well. The more that you train your dog, the easier it is to teach him something new. Essentially the dog learns how to learn. Learning a trick is just as helpful for this process as learning how to retrieve or sit and stay on command. In addition, tricks provide some amusement for you and the rest of the family.

"The world was conquered through the understanding of dogs; the world exists through the understanding of dogs."
— Friedrich Nietzsche

DOG COMPETITIONS

Training Champion Dogs

It takes a lot of work and a lot of time to raise a champion dog. By far the largest percentage of puppies in a litter end up as pets — breeders feel lucky if they get one great puppy in a litter.

Most dogs are never shown after completing a championship. A few of the very best continue to be shown as "specials", which is a class at a dog show for the top "top dogs." Basically, there are two main competitions: conformation and obedience. To understand these terms and more, here is a brief explanation of the Canadian dog show world.

Conformation:

Purebreds are simply good dogs that are continually copied, with the best ones selected for breeding. Originally, such dogs were chosen for their performance of a function (hunting, herding, sledding) and conformation classes evolved from selecting the best-looking dogs at the working events.

How does conformation work? The CKC has a book of official standards for each breed. Your dog is judged against these standards for qualities like stance, soundness, movement and type. The better conditioned and presented your dog is, the better it will do. On page 158 is a chart, originally published in *Dogs in Canada* Magazine, that explains the levels of conformation competition.

Obedience:

Obedience trials have been held in North America since the late 1930s. There are three levels, or tests, offered in obedience trials. In order to win an obedience title, a dog must qualify three times at each level and pass each exercise of the test. The three levels are:
1. Novice ("CD" or "Companion Dog")
2. Open ("CDX" or "Companion Dog Excellent")
3. Utility ("UD" or "Utility Dog"; a dog winning a UD may also be called an "OT Ch" or "Obedience Trial Champion")

Q: Why should you wear boots to a pet show?

A: You might step in a poodle.

Each level of obedience has a number of tests, as follows:

1. Novice
- heeling on- and off-leash
- standing for examination from a stranger
- recall off-leash (approximately 40 feet)
- sit-stay for 1 minute and down-stay for 3 minutes (performed in a line-up)

2. Open
- heeling off-leash
- drop on recall (during recall, dog must drop instantly on hand or voice signal — whichever the judge demands)
- retrieving a dumbbell on the flat and over a high jump
- broad jump (all jumps relative to dog's size)
- sit-stay 3 minutes, down-stay 5 minutes (handlers out of sight)

3. Utility
Utility exercises are extremely difficult. Approximately one in three dogs tested will pass.
- seek back (dog finds and returns a glove dropped by the handler during heeling)
- scent discrimination (wooden, metal and leather articles) — dog finds from among 15 identical articles the one touched by the handler
- signal exercise (dog has to heel, stand, stay, drop-sit and come from 40 feet)
- directed jumping (dog has to run out from handler approximately 40 feet, stop when told and return to owner by jumping over either a high jump or a bar jump)
- group exercise — a long stand (three minutes minimum) as judge examines dog, as in conformation judging

The very best dogs will have both a conformation championship in front of their name and an obedience or other working title following their name (i.e. CH. Rosie U.D.)

Junior handling classes are competitions for eight to 16 year-olds, showing their abilities to exhibit a dog for conformation. Andrea Blacker, a member of the Junior Kennel Club of Vancouver (see also "Kids & Dogs") won the CKC's national Junior Handler award in 1994. Junior obedience is in its infancy and should be offered at obedience trials soon.

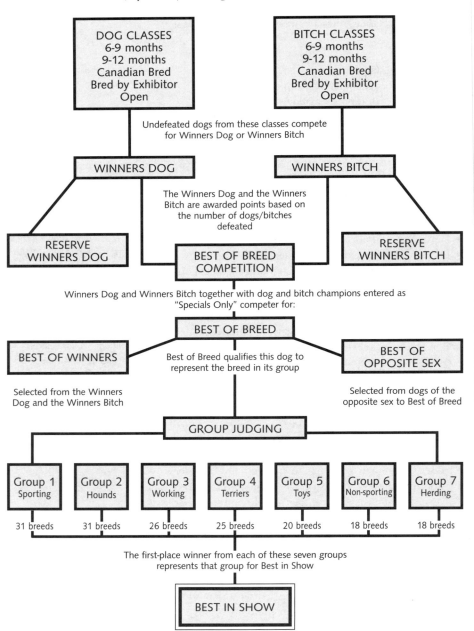

DOG CLASSES
6-9 months
9-12 months
Canadian Bred
Bred by Exhibitor
Open

BITCH CLASSES
6-9 months
9-12 months
Canadian Bred
Bred by Exhibitor
Open

Undefeated dogs from these classes compete
for Winners Dog or Winners Bitch

WINNERS DOG

WINNERS BITCH

The Winners Dog and the Winners
Bitch are awarded points based on
the number of dogs/bitches
defeated

**RESERVE
WINNERS DOG**

**BEST OF BREED
COMPETITION**

**RESERVE
WINNERS BITCH**

Winners Dog and Winners Bitch together with dog and bitch champions entered as
"Specials Only" competer for:

BEST OF BREED

BEST OF WINNERS

Best of Breed qualifies this dog to
represent the breed in its group

**BEST OF
OPPOSITE SEX**

Selected from the Winners
Dog and the Winners Bitch

Selected from dogs of the
opposite sex to Best of Breed

GROUP JUDGING

Group 1 Sporting	Group 2 Hounds	Group 3 Working	Group 4 Terriers	Group 5 Toys	Group 6 Non-sporting	Group 7 Herding
31 breeds	31 breeds	26 breeds	25 breeds	20 breeds	18 breeds	18 breeds

The first-place winner from each of these seven groups
represents that group for Best in Show

BEST IN SHOW

At the end of the show, the dog declared BIS stands undefeated
by any other dog in this show.
There is also an Altered Class for spayed and neutered dogs.

Here are the names of the various conformation and obedience trials:

	CONFORMATION	OBEDIENCE
Most elementary level	Fun Match	Correction Match
Practice matches for clubs, officials and exhibitors (sanctioned by CKC)	Sanction	Sanction
CKC-sponsored titles won at these events	Championships	Licensed Obedience Trials

If you are interested in having your purebred dog involved in conformation or obedience competition, contact your breeder or your breed club for information.

Dog Show Companies

There are three companies in British Columbia that put on dog shows:

Classic Show Services
Carol Garvin
Box 86
Maple Ridge
462-8535

Professional Dog Show Services
Sheila Paddon and Bev Atchison
23039 - 75th Ave.
Langley
888-0704 or 856-8017
website: http://www.alphagate.com/pkc

Western Dog Shows Ltd.
Kamloops
(250) 573-3944
e-mail: WesternDogShows@compupets.com
website: http://www.compupets.com/westerndogshows
   /index.html#top

The biggest dog show in Canada is the annual Lower Mainland Dog Fanciers of BC Club at the Tradex in Abbotsford. It takes place during the last weekend in October.

You can find out about upcoming shows through *Dogs in Canada* magazine, through the breed clubs and often through your vet or local pet food store. Also, try these websites:

http://www.alphagate.com/pkc

http://www.compupets.com/westerndogshows/
index.html#top

JUST FOR FUN: DOG SPORTS

Breed-specific Sports

Draft Dog Tests

Breed clubs for Newfoundlands, Bernese Mountain Dogs, English Mastiffs and Saint Bernards take part. The tests are a series of exercises with the dogs harnessed and hitched to a cart. They have to go through a series of maneuvers and do a freight haul. All of this is off-lead and by command only. To become involved, contact the breed clubs.

Field Trial Clubs

Most field trial club members are serious conservationists and are often members of organizations such as Ducks Unlimited and the BC Federation of Wildlife. Here's a list of such clubs in the Lower Mainland.

British Columbia All-breed Pointer Club
Vilma Folli
855-7290
Open to all CKC recognized pointing breeds: English Pointer, Griffon (Wire-haired Pointing) Pointer, German Short-haired Pointer, German Wire hair, English Setter, Gordon setter, Brittany spaniel, Vizsla (Smooth-haired) and Weimaraner. Organizes the annual Chukar championships (named for the Chukar bird). Two field trials a year and field dog tests.

British Columbia Amateur Field Trial Club
Jane Spearing
946-8812
Holds trials to test retrieving ability on land and water.

British Columbia Gun Dog Club Inc.
Tracey Fiddler
533-8974
Oldest retriever trial club in North America (started just after WWII).

The Great Canadian Pet Fair is held the last weekend in May at the Plaza of Nations. This is a great event with dogs, cats, even ferrets and hedgehogs. Lots of displays and shows (the Hot Dogs do agility, there is Musical Canine Freestyle and lots more). The beneficiary of the net profits from the Dog Jog and the Dog's Breakfast is BC Pets and Friends.

BC Labrador Retriever Club (1995) Society
Holly Matheson
795-2574
website: http://users.uniserve.com/~matheson/
Newsletter: *B.C.L.R.C. (1995) Society Newsletter*
Breed rescue. Information package available. Supports responsible Labrador ownership. Various members show, do field trials, hunt tests and obedience tests, or are general pets. Offers public education at the Sportsmen Show in the fall and a family picnic in the summer.

Northwest Labrador Retrievers and Water Fowlers Club
Randy Blanchard
Maple Ridge
467-3579
Trains Labrador Retrievers for field trials, hunt tests (designed as an actual day's hunt, competing against a standard) and all levels of bird hunting, including water fowling and upland game hunting.

Richmond Retriever Club
Susan Shearer
882-8408
Puts on retriever trials and holds seminars.

See also Golden Retriever Club of BC in list of breed clubs under "Finding your Dog." They do hunt tests and working certificate tests.

Lure Coursing
— Canadian Sighthound Field Association
Sighthounds were originally bred to hunt many types of game, from small rabbits to large wolves and deer. Put simply, lure coursing is a simulation of the chase. Two or three hounds of the same breed, selected by random draw, line up at the start line and, on the signal from the Huntmaster, are simultaneously "hand-slipped" by the handlers. The dogs follow an erratic course and are judged not only on speed, but on enthusiasm for the lure and the chase, ability to follow (chasing directly behind the lure and not cutting corners), agility (cornering ability, sure-footedness etc.) and endurance (not flagging at the end of the course).

The hounds are judged by two qualified judges and the one that crosses the finish line first is not always the winner. Courses are set up over a large area and can range from 400 to 1,500 yards in length. The length of the course, the length of the straightaways, the sharpness of the turns and the terrain, as well as many other factors, are variables used in designing the "hunt."

Equipment requirements are a lure machine, pulleys, line and a lure. The lure machine reels in the line at speeds up to and above 40 miles per hour. At the end of the line is the lure — usually white plastic streamers — which the hounds chase. Pulleys are placed in the ground and the line is strung around them, permitting the lure to change directions and thereby simulating the turns made by live prey. Each hound runs twice (unless dismissed, excused or disqualified for interference) and all the scores are posted for exhibitors to see. Placements are awarded for first through fifth (called NBQ or Next Best Qualified) and points for a Field Championship are awarded to the top four hounds in each stake (breed).

Only purebred Afghan Hounds, Basenji, Borzoi, Scottish Deerhounds, Ibizan Hounds, Irish Wolfhounds, Greyhounds, Pharaoh Hounds, Saluki and Whippets one year of age or older and registered with the Canadian or American kennel clubs may enter lure field trails. Spayed females, altered males and those with show ring disqualifications may also compete.

Canadian Sighthound Field Association
Bonnie Goebel
856-4763
Promotes lure coursing in Canada.

Road Trials
Dalmatian Club of Canada
Leslie Schreuder
465-0381
Currently for Dalmatians only. The dogs must go through three vet checks to complete competitions. A handler is on a horse the entire time, as is the judge. To start with, the dogs go into a field to do obedience work, which includes: a hawk exercise — a heeling exercise in a hawk position which means a maximum of one horse length

between the dog and horse); distraction — dog on leash with handler walks towards judge while dog remains in hawk position; sit or down-stay (and remain for 1 minute); speed over varying distances — dog keeps pace with or exceeds the horse's speed. As soon as the obedience trial is over, competitors move onto Endurance: trail riding over 12.5 miles or 25 miles to earn the title Road Dog (RD, for 12.5 miles) or Road Dog Excellence (RDX, for 25 miles).

Schutzhund (Protection Dog)
— German Shepherd Schutzhund Club of Canada

The concept of Schutzhund evolved around 90 years ago in Europe, when concerned owners set up a training and testing program for privately owned, working dogs. The dogs were to be able to use all their capabilities and thus the owners were able to reap the benefits of the training as well as valuable clues for selecting a good breeding specimen. The dogs and their handlers work as a team in the three categories of the Schutzhund program: Tracking, Obedience and Protection.

The exercises have changed slightly and, depending on the Schutzhund degree, consist of the following:

Tracking: The dog must retrace the path of a person (400-1500 yards with two to four turns) after 20 to 60 minutes have elapsed and be able to find two or three lost articles, regardless of weather conditions.

Obedience: The dog must follow its master's orders to heel, jump, retrieve over a 6-foot wall and send-away, both on and off leash. The dog must not be intimidated by any distractions, including the sound of a gun or a group of strangers milling about.

Protection: The dog must, without handler assistance, respond properly in critical situations, like finding and warning its master of a hidden person, preventing an assault on its handler and stopping the villain from escaping. The dog must distinguish between a harmless bystander and a potentially dangerous person. It must display courage but quit on its own when the agitator gives up.

Schutzhund training is a sport open to dogs of all working breeds, including mixed, if they can do the work. Traditionally, German Shepherds, Boxers, Dobermans,

Rottweillers, Airedales, Bouviers and Giant Schnauzers have been the most common types of dogs trained, with the German Shepherds outnumbering them all.

There are many dog owners who object to Schutzhund training and recount the experiences they have had with unqualified attack-dog trainers. These people do not wish to share their house/community with a potentially dangerous dog. It is important to remember that any large dog is potentially dangerous. The large dog needs to be handled by a responsible, knowledgeable person who will give it a lot of understanding, affection, love and attention. Anyone who lacks these basics should not even consider owning a dog — and definitely should not own one of the working breeds.

For the responsible, private working-dog owner, however, the Schutzhund sport has proven to be an ideal program. Training can be done in very small groups, training locations are readily available, time requirements are reasonable and benefits are obvious. Knowing how a dog behaves in critical situations is reassuring and provides better control over the animal, eliminating, in fact, so-called viciousness. The result is a happy, friendly but alert, controllable family dog that becomes an asset, not a nuisance or a danger, to society.

Q: What dogs need glasses?

A: Cock-eyed Spaniels.

Schutzhund Clubs

Lower Mainland German Shepherd Dog Club
Dave Jantzen
Surrey
574-0054

Richmond German Shepherd Shutzhund Club of BC
Jeff Olsen
Richmond
241-8522

West Coast German Shepherd Schutzhund Club
Rita Mutcher
Langley
534-0172

Western Rescue Schutzhund Club
Sue Saunders
Surrey
590-2558

Sheepdog Herding

BC Stockdog Association (Lower Mainland Chapter)
Bruce McLeod
590-6097
Information on herding breeds (primarily Border Collies, Australian Shepherds and Kelpies). Trains working-stock dogs to compete in and host monthly handy-dog trials, and sponsors open trials to work the dogs. Also sponsors clinics. Works on maintaining and improving the breed. Works with farmers and ranchers to improve the handling of their dogs and tries to promote the use of dogs in agriculture as being cost effective.

Herding/Sheep Dog Trials
Bill McCallum
462-8088
(or Anne Martin and Bev Achison: 590-4529)
Participates in the Annual Borderline Sheepdog Trial, which usually occurs during the second-last weekend of June. An excellent spectator sport — and it's free. About 50 to 70 dogs compete. Handlers come from Alberta and all over the Pacific Northwest. Call for information on the location of the trial.

Water Trials
Exercises designed to show off what the dogs were originally bred to do. Primarily for Newfoundlands and Portuguese Water Dogs (the rules are different for each breed, but the principle is the same). The Portuguese Water Dog clubs haven't held a trial in Canada yet, but plan to do so once sanctioned by the Portuguese Water Dog Club of America. Contact the breed clubs to get involved.

City folk with a sheep dog and nothing to herd? No problem — you can rent a flock. John Carter runs Herder's Haven (19022 - 16th Ave., Surrey; 541-8739). He started the business because there were so many Border Collies that never saw stock, and people wanted to give it a try. John knows his herding dogs, and he is also involved with the collie eye anomaly program for eye testing and mating. John also works his dogs with animals other than sheep — he's hired by golf clubs to round up Canada Geese. He can also seen at demonstrations, where his dogs herd Indian Runner ducks.

All-breed Sports

Agility

— *Agility Association of Canada*

Dog Agility began in England in 1974, as a half-time show for the prestigious Crufts Dog Show. By 1988, many trials were being held and agility had become a truly distinct sport. Since then, the sport has spread around the world to the rest of Europe, Australia and North America. In 1986, the United States Dog Agility Association (USDAA) was formed. Two years later, Art Newman of Ottawa founded the Agility Association of Canada (AAC) to promote national standards for agility competition.

The sport is open to all dog breeds, both purebred and those with, shall we say, a Heinz-57 pedigree. All dogs and their handlers compete on an equal footing and are judged entirely upon performance. It does require a level of physical fitness and not all breeds are well suited for it because of their physical builds. The fastest, most flawless dog and handler win. Not only is there no distinction between the dog breeds but men, women and children also compete against one another as equals. Dog agility is very much a family affair, providing entertainment, good-natured rivalry, exercises and a great excuse for a family outing.

At the competitive level, agility is much like the equestrian events from which it was derived. A course is comprised of a series of obstacles such as jumps, tunnels, see-saws, "A" frames and other objects. The handlers give direction and guidance to their dogs. The performance is judged, and infractions such as knocked-down bars, taking too long to complete the course and not touching the contact zones result in faults being assessed in accordance with AAC rules. Dogs are placed in one of four divisions, determined by their shoulder height, and compete against others in that division. The winner is the dog with the least number of faults. In the case of a tie, the dog with the fastest time wins.

Dog Play

http://www.dog-play.com/ is a terrific site, with loads of links to the following activities:

Agility, Animal Assisted Therapy, Animal Assisted Activities, Carting, Coursing and racing, Dog Camps, Activity Sampler: Education, Earthdog Trials, Eventing, Flygility, Flyball, Flying Disc, Herding, Hiking, Backpacking and Dog Walks, Hunt and Field Trials, Kids and Dogs, Obedience, Performance Art (Tricks), Pet Facilitated Therapy, Precision Drill Teams, Pulling, Rollerblade, Search and Rescue, Skijoring, Sledding, Socializing and Off-leash Play, Tracking, Training, Weight Pulling, and Visiting Pets.

Here are the AAC's height standards:

Jump Height	Dog Height
12 inches	12 inches & under
18 inches	16 inches & under
24 inches	21 inches & under
30 inches	over 21 inches

Agility Clubs

Agility Association Of Canada (AAC)
Debbie Maillet
R.R.#6
Moncton, New Brunswick
E1C 8K1
local contact: Dee Gleed
533-0197
e-mail: D._Gleed@bc.sympatico.ca

Camrose Kennels
4806 - 168th St.
Surrey
576-6547
Agility training by Margaret Warren on Tuesdays, Wednesdays and Thursdays.

Dog Star Canine Sports Club
Wesley Barnaby
Tri-Star Stables
4409 - 66th St.
Ladner
576-6681
website: http://www.citywidenet.com/barnaby/pctc.htm
Monday night classes at 7 p.m.; drop-in Friday nights at 8 p.m. Puts on demonstrations, agility trials and flyball tournaments.

Dogwood Pacesetters Canine Sports Club
Karen and Rick Palylyk
33678 Elizabeth Ave.
Abbotsford
820-0639
Newsletter: *Dogwood Tales*
Dogwood Pacesetters was formed in 1986. Involved with training and practice in agility and flyball, along with

Karen Palylyk of Viewpoint K-9 Agility Club and Dogwood Pacesetters recommends the following books on agility:
Agility is Fun (books 1 and 2), by Ruth Hobday (Our Dog Publishing Company, England);
Teaching Agility, by Peter Lewis and John Gilbert (Canine Publications, England);
Agility Workbook Series (Clean Run Publications, Massachussetts).

Karen Palylyk's favourite agility home page is: http://www.dogpatch.org/agility.html.
   This site contains an enormous amount of information and also tells you how to join a huge e-mail listserv, Cleanrun-L.

participation in public education and community functions and displays.

Jump Start Dog Agility
Dee Gleed
24202 - 56th Ave.
Langley
533-0197

K-9 Cliffhangers
Peter Savage
North Vancouver
987-1676
Savage teaches the K-9 Kapers Agility Class at the William Griffin Centre in North Vancouver. Club has weekly practices, competes in AAC competitions, does demonstrations.

Matsqui Flyball & Agility Club
Wendy Porter
Matsqui Agri Fair Building
850-8852
Newsletter: *Dog Trax*
Holds classes on Monday nights. Puts on annual flyball tournament and agility trial.

The Monday Night Gang Flyball, Agility and Scent Hurdling
Anne Martin
Valley Therapeutic Riding Association
6918 - 232nd St. South
Langley
590-4529
Drop-in classes on Wednesday nights from 8 to 10 p.m.

Viewpoint K-9 Agility Club
Karen Palylyk
33678 Elizabeth Ave.
Abbotsford
820-0639
Training club.

Photograph by Ellice Hauta

Want to build your own agility course? The AAC's rule book has all of the specifications for the obstacles, along with the rules for the game.

Den Trials
Terra Canine Den Trial Association
Carol Swan Lang
855-1720
Promoting den trials for any breed that can fit into a 9-inch tunnel. The goal is for the dogs to go through tunnels and find rats in 30 seconds, and then work at the rats (which are in cages) by barking and digging for 1 minute. This particular group was formed because the National Association is limited to terriers and dachshunds.

Flyball
— Ian Hoggs
Flyball is a team sport for dogs that was invented in California in the late 1970s. Legend has it that Herbert Wagner first showed it to millions of Americans on the *Johnny Carson Show*. Soon afterwards, dog trainers and dog clubs were making and using flyball boxes. In the early 1980s, the sport became so popular that the North American Flyball Association (NAFA) was formed and today they are the worldwide authority for flyball.

Flyball is a relay race with four dogs on a team. The course consists of a starting line, four hurdles spaced 10 feet apart and a box. The first hurdle is 6 feet from the start line and the box is 15 feet from the last hurdle, for a 51-foot overall length. Each dog jumps the hurdles and steps on a spring-loaded box that shoots out a tennis ball. The dog catches the tennis ball and then runs back over the four hurdles. (The height of the hurdles is dependent on the height of the dogs in the team — 4 inches below the shoulder height of the shortest dog. Eight inches is the minimum height and 16 inches is the maximum height.) When the first dog crosses the starting line, the next dog goes. The first team to have all four dogs run without errors wins the heat.

Tournaments are usually organized in either a double elimination or round robin format. Double elimination is usually best of three or best of five. Round robin is usually best three out of five and the first team to win three heats receives one point towards their standing in the tournament.

Best book on Flyball training, recommended by Val Culpin, Flyball judge and member Board of Directors, North American Flyball Association: *Flyball Training...Start to Finish* by Jacqueline Parkin (Alpine). Two hundred pages with lots of photos.

Flyball Clubs

Camrose Kings Flyball Team
Peter Warren
Camrose Kennels
4806 - 168th St.
Surrey
576-6547
Flyball on Fridays and Saturdays.

Canine Caretakers
Evelyn Bliss
270-0309
Agility, flyball, obedience, conformation handling, behavioural counselling and herbal consulting.

Dog Star Canine Sports Club
Wesley Barnaby
Tri-Star Stables
4409 - 66th St.
Ladner
576-6681
website: http://www.citywidenet.com/barnaby/pctc.htm
Monday night classes 7 p.m.; drop-in Friday nights 8 p.m. Demonstrations, agility trials and flyball tournaments.

Dogwood Pacesetters Canine Sports Club
Karen and Rick Palylyk
33678 Elizabeth Ave.
Abbotsford
(604) 820-0639
Newsletter: *Dogwood Tales*
Dogwood Pacesetters originated in 1986. Involved with training and practice of agility and flyball activities, participation in public education, and community functions and displays. Also does drill-team precision patterns to music. Have done grand openings to events and parade drills. These involve 12 handlers in uniforms, with their dogs and holding flags. A high level of obedience is required for drill team membership.

Photograph by Ellice Hauta

The fastest recorded flyball time is 16.75 seconds. It was clocked by the Jets team from Southhampton, England.

Fur Flies
Dee Gleed
24202 - 56th Ave.
Langley
533-0197
A loose group from Langley, Surrey, Richmond and Abbotsford. Bi-weekly sessions. Train wherever they can and have two teams. In it for the fun.

Matsqui Flyball & Agility Club
Wendy Porter
Matsqui Agri Fair Building
850-8852
Newsletter: *Dog Trax*
Holds classes on Monday nights. Puts on annual flyball tournament and agility trial.

The Monday Night Gang Flyball and Agility
Anne Martin
Valley Therapeutic Riding Association
6918 - 232nd St. South
Langley
590-4529
Drop-in classes on Wednesday nights from 8 to 10 p.m.

The North Shore Flyers Flyball Club
Shirley Sanderson
925-3167
Flyball classes on Saturday mornings at the Navy League Building in Mahon Park, through the North Vancouver Recreation Commission. Once the classes are completed, you can join the club, which has weekly training sessions. Teams compete in tournaments. Hosts an annual July tournament.

Pacific Canine Training Centre
Wesley Barnaby
4409 - 66th St.
Ladner
576-6681
Their business is training in agility and flyball.

Richmond Huggables Flyball Team
Evelyn Bliss
270-0309
Flyball for all bull breeds (Bull Terriers, American Bull Dogs, Staffordshire Terriers).

Ridge Runners Flyball Club
Dianna Kirkwood
Maple Ridge
462-0056
Practice Tuesday evenings, hold annual tournament, present demos and compete.

Toonies
Elsie May Lang
Coquitlam
421-4927
website: http://www.holesome.com/holesomekennels/
e-mail: holesome@uniserve.com
Flyball classes Monday nights in Blue Mountain Park and Sunday nights at the Equestrian Centre in Burnaby

Flyball home page:
http://www.cs.umn.edu/
~ianhogg/flyball/
flyball.html
(loaded with links and illustrated with a great animation of a dog playing flyball).

Scent Hurdling
The Monday Night Gang Scent Hurdling
Anne Martin
Valley Therapeutic Riding Association
6918 - 232nd St. South
Langley
590-4529
Scent Hurdling involves four jumps with a platform at the end which holds two dumbbells for each dog on the team. The dogs have to grab their own dumbbell (by scent) and head back to the start. Limited to purebred dogs. Drop-in classes on Wednesday nights.

Tracking
Tracking Classes
Gary and Shirley Roe
Cloverdale
574-5937
Also do obedience.

Superdogs at the PNE first brought flyball and agility to the Vancouver area.

Weight-pulling
International Weight Pull Association (IWPA)
Darla Williams
532-1230
Comes to Vancouver twice a year for competitions. All breeds welcome. The dogs are harnessed to a sled system loaded with weights. The winner pulls a certain amount of weight over a certain distance in the fastest time.

Dog-sport Exhibitions

Hot Dogs
Wesley Barnaby
576-6681
Organized to put on demonstrations of flyball and agility at the Great Canadian Pet Fairs and charitable community events.

Superdogs
e-mail: pawprints@tvo.org
website: http://www.pawprints.com/clients/superdogs/
    superdogs.html
You may have seen them at the Pacific National Exhibition. Superdogs is a dog entertainment show purely for fun, and is where most folks around here first saw agility. Participation is by invitation only. The original Superdog was Musketeer, a black Labrador-German Shepherd cross from Surrey that, about 18 years ago, performed the show with only one hip. Musketeer's owner, Anne Martin, is still involved with Superdogs.

Musical Canine Sports

What are Musical Canine Sports? Dancing with dogs — and this isn't fiction! Musical Canine Sports was invented in Abbotsford and has taken off in the United States. It is very hard to visualize, so don't ever pass up an opportunity to see this terrific dog sport. It's fun, entertaining and challenging.

Musical Freestyle
— Musical Canine Sports International (MCSI)

Musical freestyle gives new meaning to having a partner with two left feet — actually, two left feet, two right feet, a tail and a hairy back. (Good thing your dance partner is supposed to be a dog!) Musical freestyle is a blending of dog obedience and dance that presents a visually exciting display of handler and canine teamwork. The handler and dog perform dance-oriented footwork in time to the music, rather than displaying the traditional walking pace of obedience. Heeling is an important component of freestyle but non-standard movements are also expected to be displayed by the dog, along with attention and enthusiasm. The movements have a degree of difficulty over and above that normally seen in the obedience ring.

Musical freestyle is a competitive sport. Dance teams are judged and are awarded higher points for more difficult moves. Those moves can include weaving backwards through the handlers' legs, mid-air flips and jumping over the handler. Teams are penalized for dangerous moves and a dog must never be lifted higher than the handler's shoulders. A variety of handler upper-body movements are encouraged to lend interpretation to the music and the handler freely uses the body, arms, and legs. Footwork is a mixture of dance-related steps and traditional movements at different

> "If you eliminate smoking and gambling, you will be amazed to find that almost all an Englishman's pleasures can be, and mostly are, shared by his dog."
> — George Bernard Shaw

speeds. Handlers are encouraged to wear costumes to match the theme of the music, but the dogs are not allowed to wear costumes. Throughout the three- to five-minute routine, the handler may encourage the dog's performance with verbal commands, but no training aids or foods of any kind are permitted in the competition ring.

Teams can compete as individuals, pairs or groups and in the on-leash or off-leash divisions. Any kind of dog can compete in this fun and increasingly popular sport.

Call to find out when the next local demo will be held.

Musical Freestyle in BC
Bonnie Backosti
856-6500
or Val Culpin
504-7661
or Carol Swan Lang
855-1720
web sites: http://www.compupets.com/lmdf/
    musical.htm#top
http://www.woofs.org/cycle/freestyle/frstyl.html

Photograph by
Kent Southwell

VI. At Home, On the Road & At Work with Your Dog

It's all very fine to want a dog, but where are you going to park your pooch once you have it? Finding a place to live in Vancouver is tough enough, but finding a place that will take you and your dog is even more difficult. Folks at the BC SPCA are working on a solution for responsible pet owners; included in this chapter is information about their proposals as well as legal information on the Condominium Act. And what about those times when you are planning to be away for a day or a week? Doggie Day Cares can offer a short-term solution — and some dogs go every day, even when their owners are in town, returning fit, all played out and content. There are also dozens of kennels around the Lower Mainland, and there are many dog sitters too.

If you are travelling with your dog, you may want to check our list of hotels and motels that accept pets before setting out. This chapter also offers a glimpse into the world of working dogs — and it's a fascinating world. As this information shows, lot of dogs really love to work, whether by acting in a movie, guiding a person with a disability, busting a drug dealer going through customs or tracking a criminal.

A HOME FOR YOU AND YOUR DOG

Rental Accommodation

— Stephan Huddart, British Columbia SPCA

Every day, the calls come in to the SPCA shelters. Some callers are angry, some are grief-stricken, and all want help. . .

"I just moved here from Toronto with my small dog and I want to know if you have the same law here that says landlords can't discriminate against people who have a pet."

"My client is disabled and her pet is her only companion. She's desperate. Is there a list of rental housing that accepts people with pets?"

"My children and I have two small, well-behaved dogs. Four months ago our landlord died and we were given six months to find new accommodation. I've called dozens of ads with no luck and now I'm looking at having to give the dogs up. How am I ever going to explain this to the kids?"

Clearly, there is a problem here. While over half of BC homeowners have pets, only five percent of rental housing allows animals. The result of this policy is seen at SPCA shelters, where an estimated 15 percent of surrendered animals are given up because owners cannot find rental housing. Province-wide, that adds up to thousands of animals a year, only half of whom will find homes.

Seniors are especially vulnerable — upon moving into smaller, multi-unit housing after the death of a spouse, many find that their beloved cat or dog must be given up. In addition to added loss, they face lonely futures, their days bereft of the consoling companionship of a pet.

The benefits of pet ownership have been well-documented. During the past decade, studies have found that companion animals assist children with the development of language skills, responsibility and self-esteem. Elderly people with pets are less likely to suffer depression, and record fewer doctors' visits. Heart surgery patients with pets recover more quickly that those without. Is it fair to deny these and other benefits to people just because they cannot afford their own homes?

"Love me, love my dog."
— John Heywood

On the other hand, property owners and managers have legitimate concerns too, and it seems that every landlord has a horror story about animals damaging apartments and terrorizing tenants. Unfortunately, it is the irresponsible actions of the few that create hardship for the responsible majority.

Ontario passed a law in 1990 prohibiting the eviction of tenants just because they had pets. In the United States, legislation is in place allowing seniors in federally funded housing to have pets. San Francisco SPCA's Open Door Program educates landlords and tenants as to each other's needs, providing detailed guidelines for both groups and a mediation service when conflicts arise. In British Columbia, the BC Housing Commission, with 7,000 units under management, developed a successful pet owner policy several years ago with the help of the British Columbia SPCA and the British Columbia Veterinary Medical Association. A recent review confirmed that the policy is working well.

The BC SPCA has been working on this issue together with the Residential Tenancy Branch, the Rental Housing Council, the BC Veterinary Medical Association and tenants groups. A proposal outlining an education program for landlords and tenants has received approval in principle from the Rental Council, and work is now proceeding on an ancillary insurance program whereby responsible pet owners will be able to indemnify their landlords against pet-caused damage. We hope to begin a pilot program by the end of 1997. With continued pressure and support from the public, and the cooperation of the animal welfare community, we can look forward to seeing fewer "No Pets Allowed" signs and more that read "Responsible Pet Owners Welcome."

The following tips for people seeking rental accommodation are suggested by the Regina Humane Society:

- Have references ready that mention your pet specifically. Show signs of being responsible. Have proof of licensing, spaying/neutering, surgery, vaccinations, regular veterinary care, obedience school training etc.
- Encourage the landlord to meet your freshly groomed, well-behaved pet.

> "I loathe people who keep dogs. They are cowards who haven't got the guts to bite people themselves."
> — August Strindberg,
> *A Madman's Diary*

- Offer to pay an additional pet deposit.
- Show a willingness to have the landlord visit your place shortly after rental so he or she feels satisfied the pet is adjusting.
- Agree to sign a pet agreement; offer to cover any damages made by your pet.
- Upon meeting the landlord for the first time, dress as if you were in a job interview. Dressing well shows you care about how you take care of yourself, your living environment, and your pet.

If you're looking for more information, another good resource is put together by *Cynophilist* (Latin for "dog lover") Catherine Willet. When she moved here from Montreal, Willet was shocked to discover how difficult it was to find dog-friendly apartments. Determined to keep Internet, her SPCA Border Collie mix, Willet moved three times in one year before finding a place that met the needs of her human and canine family. She produces a list (updated monthly) of Vancouver apartment buildings that accept dogs. Anyone knowing of dog-friendly buildings is urged to add addresses to the list. As well, help distributing the newsletter throughout Vancouver is always welcome. To contribute to the list or to obtain a copy, send a self-addressed stamped envelope to:

P.O. Box 3995
VMPO
Vancouver
V6B 3Z4
e-mail: cwillet@vcn.bc.ca

Recommended Reading: Condominium Law and Practice in British Columbia, by Margaret Fairweather and Lynn Ramsay (Continuing Legal Education Society of British Columbia, 1996).

The Condo Act

— *Margaret Fairweather and Lynn Ramsay*
(from *Condominium Law and Practice in British Columbia*, 1996)

When you buy a condominium, there are all sorts of regulations and restrictions built into your strata council by-laws — but there is little in condominium owning that can create as much controversy as restricting animals. A strata corporation can't prohibit the ownership of a dog or a cat unless it is specifically stated in the by-laws, and they can't restrict pet ownership retroactively. The restriction on "all pets" has been overturned by an Ontario court because such a by-law would include pets like goldfish, which hardly interfere with the use and enjoyment of a strata lot or common property.

One solution to the "pet" issue is to give the strata corporation discretion, after close observation of the size,

Portrait by
Leah MacFarlane

type and behaviour of the pet, to enter into a pet license agreement with the owner. The pet license agreement, to which the by-laws may refer, identifies the pet by photograph and grants the owner a license to keep the pet under certain conditions. Those conditions impose restrictions on the pet's behaviour. The agreement provides for fines, termination for cause and an indemnity from the owner for damage the pet may cause to common property or other strata lots.

Because of the contentious nature of this topic, strata councils are encouraged to act carefully in establishing rules that are fair and reasonable. It is recommended that they talk to other strata councils, gather examples of successful by-laws and discuss it all with a lawyer. Also, they should consult with the Condominium Home Owners' Association of BC (584-2462).

TRAVELLING WITH YOUR DOG

Hotels and Motels

Thankfully, these days there are many hotels and motels that will let you stay with your pet. Often hotels will accept pets but do not want to advertise this policy. Call your favourite hotel and find out what they allow. When you are travelling, also consult the American Automobile Association (AAA) tome, *PETBOOK: Accommodations Offering Facilities For Your Pet*. The following hotels welcome pets openly. If you come across other places that will take dogs — in Vancouver as well as the rest of BC and Washington State, please let us know.

Burnaby
Lake City Motor Inn
5415 Lougheed Hwy.
V5B 2Z7
294-5331
Small pets only. $5

Coquitlam
Coquitlam Sleepy Lodge
730 Clarke Rd.
V3J 3Y1
937-7737 or 1-800-667-5955
All pets; no big dogs. $10

Delta
Best Western Tsawassen Inn
1665-56th St.
V4L 2B2
All dogs — some rules and restrictions apply.

Langley
Langley Motor Inn
21653 Fraser Hwy.
V3A 4H1
533-4431
Only take clean dogs. $5

West Country Hotel
20222 - 56th Ave.
V3A 3Y5
530-5121

Westward Inn
19650 Fraser Hwy.
V3A 4C7
534-9238
All dogs and pets. $4

Maple Ridge

Travelodge Maple Ridge
21650 Lougheed Hwy.
V2X 2S1
467-1511
$50 deposit required; no other charges.

North Vancouver

Lynnwood Inn
1515 Barrow St.
V2J 1B7
988-6161

Richmond

Best Western Richmond Inn & Convention Center
7551 Westminster Hwy.
V6X 1A3
273-7878

Delta Pacific Resort and Conference Centre
10251 St. Edwards Dr.
V6X 2M9
278-9611
Small pets welcome.

Delta Vancouver Airport Hotel & Marina
3500 Cessna Dr.
V7B 1C7
278-1241
Small pets welcome.

Service with a smile

A man wrote a letter to a small hotel in a midwest town he planned to visit on his vacation. He wrote: "I would very much like to bring my dog with me. He is well-groomed and very well behaved. Would you be willing to permit me to keep him in my room with me at night?" An immediate reply came from the hotel owner, who said: "I've been operating this hotel for many years. In all that time, I've never had a dog steal towels, bed clothes or silverware or pictures off the walls. I've never had to evict a dog in the middle of the night for being drunk and disorderly. And I've never had a dog run out on a hotel bill. Yes, indeed, your dog is welcome at my hotel. And, if your dog will vouch for you, you're welcome to stay here, too."
— Karl Albrect and Ron Zenke, Service America

Stay 'n' Save Motor Inn
10551 St. Edwards Dr.
V6X 3L8
273-3311
Small pets only.

Vancouver

Coast Vancouver Airport Hotel
1041 S.W. Marine Dr.
V6P 6L6
263-1555
Small pets only. $20 surcharge; $200 deposit if no credit card.

The Georgian Court Hotel
773 Beatty St.
V6B 2M4
682-5555
Small pets only.

Four Seasons Hotel
791 W. Georgia St.
V6C 2T4
689-9333
This hotel not only takes dogs, they have a "Dog Recognition Program." As well, a dog amenity is delivered to patrons on a silver tray. This amenity is a handmade dog bowl (adorned with the hotel logo and doggie designs, created by local ceramic artist Georgina Brandon) filled with homemade dog biscuits and accompanied by an additional doggie bowl filled with Evian water. A recipe card for the biscuits is included, along with a rose. There is a dog bed available on request and the concierge will also walk the dog on request.

Holiday Inn, Vancouver Centre
711 W. Broadway
V5Z 3Y2
879-0551
Will take one animal under 40 pounds.

Holiday Inn Hotel & Suites, Vancouver Downtown
1110 Howe St.
V6Z 1R2
684-2151

The London Guard Motel
2227 Kingsway
V5N 2T6
430-4646
Small pets only. $2.

2400 Motel
2400 Kingsway
V5R 5G9
434-2464
Maximum two dogs per unit. $4 per unit.

YMCA Hotel
955 Burrard St.
V6Z 1Y2
681-0221
Well-kept dogs. $10.

Dogs on BC Ferries

Pets must remain inside a vehicle (not, for example, in the box of a pick-up truck) throughout the entire journey. Walk-on passengers with dogs will be directed to board onto the vehicle deck and must securely tether the dog in an area away from all cars and other passengers. Owners must clean up after the animal. The corporation carries no liability. The only dogs allowed on the passenger deck are seeing-eye dogs or dogs required for disabled people.

Crossing the Border

All your dog needs to cross the border into the United States is an updated rabies shot. The customs officer will ask for it. Other than that, it is a good idea to have a collar and ID tag, plus any certificates or registration papers in your possession.

"We travel a lot on the BC Ferries' Gulf Islands route and the dog accommodations are pitiful. You cannot take your dog above the car decks (although I have seen little puppies smuggled in). If you are travelling without a car, there are a few chairs for dog owners and a place to tie your dog right in the middle of the car deck (amid the fumes and heat). If you are travelling by car you can leave your dog in the car, but beware the heat in summer (avoid parking next to the exhaust fan if at all possible!). We always leave the windows open and risk being ripped off. I sometimes resort to standing at the back of the car deck with the dogs. There are are alot of people travelling with their dogs; it's amazing that there aren't better facilities!"
— Lori Staehling, owner of Golden Retrievers Ginger and Teddy

A Car Kit for Travelling with your Dog

Here are the essential car-kit items:
- a big towel
- bottled water
- bowl(s)
- a bag of food
- first aid kit
- in Vancouver's hot summers, some ice in a cooler

LEAVING YOUR DOG BEHIND:
KENNELS, SITTERS & DAY CARE

Kennels/Boarding

If you are going out of town and need to put your dog in a dog friendly and safe environment, a kennel is the answer. Ask your friends or your vet for recommendations, and check out a number of these places. If you live in Vancouver, you can expect to drive at least half an hour to a kennel, as they are all in the suburbs. Many kennels specialize in certain breeds, and most can also provide supplementary services such as grooming or training advice, day care, or sick care. Some will also board cats and other pets.

Aldergrove

Aldergrove Kennels
26306 - 56th Ave.
856-DOGS
664-1551
Fax: 856-5554, ext. 5027
Kennels, training and grooming.

Big Valley Kennels and Labradors
26488 - 13th Ave.
856-3092

Birch-Bark Kennels
26436 - 13th Ave.
856-4321
Board dogs, cats and all other pets. Offer day care, sick care of small pets and geriatric care.

TNT Retrievers Boarding Kennel and Training Facility
Janice Gunn
27624 Watson Rd.
857-9891
Doggy day care and boarding; also offer training.

Burnaby

Aberdeen Animal Hospital
4856 E. Hastings St.
293-1294
Grooming, full hospital services, boarding, day care. Associated with Fraserview Animal Clinic and Kerrisdale Hospital in Vancouver, and Aberdeen Kennel and Cattery in Richmond.

Kidd Kare Pet Services
329-3736
Pet taxi throughout Greater Vancouver area, day care, pick-up and delivery dogwalking, walks to beach and parks, kennel-free boarding.

Coquitlam

Dogwood Kennels
4124 Cedar St.
941-6377

Delta

Delta Kennels
4335 - 104th St.
596-0911

Gibsons

Bullock's Bowser Boarding and Cat House
Frances Bullock
886-8659
Animal health technologist. Pick up and delivery to the North Shore.

Langley

Hy-Line Kennels & Cattery
26220 - 56th Ave.
856-3560

North Vancouver

Northwest Boarding Kennels Ltd.
Dennis Brunton
1310 Monashee
985-4913
Specializes in family boarding and training.

Port Coquitlam

Countryside Kennels
558 Prairie Ave.
945-0125
Kennels, grooming, day care, obedience training.

Kendon Kennels
1185 Dominion
941-2313
Boarding and day care.

Richmond

Aberden Kennel & Cattery Ltd.
7300 No. 5 Rd.
Boarding, day care and grooming.

Alabon Country Kennels
20391 Westminster Hwy.
270-2822
Boarding, grooming, obedience training.

Belle Mode Boarding Kennels
6480 No. 7 Rd.
278-1354
Boarding and grooming.

Kidd Kare Pet Services
329-3736
Kennel-free boarding, also does day care, pick-up and delivery, walks to beach and parks, and Pet Taxi throughout Greater Vancouver area.

Pads and Paws Pet Motel
6151 No. 7 Rd.
273-8177

Richmond Kennels
1350 Blundell Rd.
273-6553
Trainer Tammy Routley speaks Japanese. Kennels for dogs and cats.

"I'm a lean dog, a keen dog, a wild dog, and lone."
— Irene Rutherford McLeod, "Lone Dog"

Rondivillls
16640 Westminster Hwy.
278-7181
Training, boarding, grooming, pet taxi, day care.

Surrey
Brynjulf Canine Services
9436 - 184th St.
882-3946
Boarding kennels, training, grooming.

Camp Critters
18030 - 32 Ave.
541-4138
Boarding and obedience training.

Camrose Kennels
4806 - 168th St.
576-6547
All-breed boarding kennel.

Canadian Institute of Professional Dog Training & Boarding Kennels
19564 - 15th Ave.
538-5529
Boarding and obedience training.

Klahanie Kennels
18718 - 32nd Ave
541-2772
Boarding, obedience and behaviour modification.

Meadow View Acres
Bonnie/Moe Ritch
4044 - 184th St.
574-2323
Grooming, training, boarding.

North American Guard Dog & Kenneling Services Ltd.
16238 - 56th St.
574-9757
Grooming, behaviour modification, training of dog trainers, kennels.

Silver Birch Kennels
4593 - 152nd St.
574-4209

White Rock Kennels Ltd.
18867 - 8th Ave.
531-2275
Close to truck border. Set on five acres; has underfloor-heated kennels.

Willchris Kennels Ltd.
14824 - 40th. Ave.
576-9603
Obedience, day care.

Vancouver
Arbutus West Animal Clinic Ltd.
2809 W. 16th
736-6701
Boards small breeds.

Fraser Pet Hospital
4305 Fraser St.
872-7671
Boarding, grooming, day care.

Hollywood North Canine Training and Talent Agency
104-1037 W. Broadway
738-1568
Boarding, day care, several levels of obedience.

I Love Dogs
Sue Laidlaw and Dawn McDonald
228-1945

Kerrisdale Veterinary Hospital Ltd.
5999 W. Blvd.
266-4171
Complete hospital facilities, grooming, boarding, day care. Connected with Fraserview Animal Clinic, Aberdeen Kennel & Cattery (Richmond), and Aberdeen Animal Hospital (Burnaby).

No, you cannot take your dog on public transit in Vancouver. Not to the vet, not to the park, not to the groomer, the trainer or to the airport. Not even in off-peak times. In Toronto, Montreal, Calgary, Edmonton, Seattle, New York — sure, take your dog; but not here, unless you have a guide dog. The transit commission was approached many times about this issue and eventually approved the idea but the driver's union didn't. They felt that there might be problems and the drivers would be responsible. It is possible that such problems might occur — but all those other cities say that there have been few problems. Let's hope for change in the future.

Kidd Kare Pet Services
329-3736
Pet taxi, day care, dogwalking, walks to beach and parks, kennel-free boarding.

Point Grey Veterenary Clinic
4362 W. 10th Ave.
228-1714
Grooming, full veterinary service, shop, training (semi-private and private lessons), boarding, day care, walking.

Vancouver Veterinary Hospital (1991) Ltd.
1541 Kingsway
876-2231
Full veterinary services, boarding.

West Vancouver
Howe Sound Pet Services Ltd.
624 Park Royal North
925-9325
Day care by the hour, boarding kennel on Bowen Island (reserve through Petstore number).

White Rock
White Rock Kennels Ltd.
18867 - 8th Ave.
531-2275
Boarding and day care.

Dog Sitters

Pet sitters come to your house while you are away during the day and/or overnight. Some combine pet sitting with caring for your house overnight or on a drop-in basis.

Aldergrove
TLC In Home Pet Sitters
856-4866
Surrey, White Rock, Langley area. Pick-up and delivery dog walking.

Burnaby
Hugs & Kisses Pet Sitters
731-1948
Home visits, home-based day care in Burnaby

The Purple Leash
Jennifer Lloyd
230-5514

Coquitlam
Luv-A-Pet
64-CARE (2273)
Pet sitting in your home, dog walking pick-up & delivery.

Delta
Custom Home Watch (and Delta Doggie Doo)
Harley Rea
220-0074
Pet care in your home, walks. Bonded.

Langley
TLC In Home Pet Sitters
856-4866
Surrey, White Rock, Langley area. Pick-up and delivery dog walking.

North Vancouver
Animal Profiles Pet Sitting
Jan Large
988-4642

Happy Pet Sitters
Sylvia
984-9477
In-home dog and pet sitting.

A much mentioned favourite dog book: *Eminent Dogs, Dangerous Men,* by Donald McCaig (Harper Collins, 1991). McCaig also wrote *Nop's Trials* (Crown Publishers, 1984) and *Nop's Hope* (Crown Publishers, 1984).

Peace of Mind Pet Services
Julie Bryson
984-7395
Pet sitters. Also do dog walking, but their specialty is pet ambulance and geriatric care.

The Pet Sitters: Personalized Nanny Care for your Pets
Teri Booth
980-0438
Home care, boards in her home, dog walking, pet taxi.

The Purple Leash
Jennifer Lloyd
230-5514

Rest Assured, Your Home Sentry and Pet Care Service
Carol Hurrell
984-2822
Dog walking and pet sitting.

Richmond

House Minders
Jan McIntyre
272-4731
Pet sitting — up to three daily visits to your home while you are away. Dog walking from your home. Reliable and affordable.

Perfect Pet Care
Deborah Wolfe
878-0364
Pet sitting, training, walking.

Surrey

Custom Home-Watch International
581-1035
Dog sitting, overnight and drop-in.

TLC In Home Pet Sitters
856-4866
Surrey, White Rock, Langley area. Pick-up and delivery dog walking. $11 once a day; $16 twice a day; less for two dogs.

Rosie's Pet Services
589-4314 or 435-6160
Pet taxi, dog walking, pet sitting.

Vancouver
The Pet Nanny
Nicole LeBlanc
899-431
Dog walking, pet sitting, pet taxi.

Paws at Home
Nicole
739-1818
Dog walking, pet sitting.

Perfect Pet Care
Deborah Wolfe
878-0364
Pet sitting, training, walking.

Pet sitting by Sandy Morris
Sandy Morris
601-0595
Insured; Veterinary Assistant experience; will do some house sitting.

TLC Pet Care in your Home
Ricardo
682-8905 or 649-0107 (cell)
Downtown, Kitsilano, False Creek.

Whiskers Pet Services
551-5041
West Side and West End
Walks in Pacific Spirit Park; pet sitting.

100% Pet Care
Leanne
879-0077
Discount professional grooming, U-groom evenings (half price of regular), dental maintenance, pick-up and delivery, pet sitting, training and problem solving.

Q: What goes "Tick-tick, woof-woof"?

A: A watch dog.

White Rock

Paws-itive Pet Sitters
Elizabeth McLeod
531-7803
At-home pet sitter; provides pet transportation.

TLC In Home Pet Sitters
856-4866
Surrey, White Rock, Langley area. Pick-up and delivery dog walking. $11 once a day, $16 twice a day, less for two dogs.

Doggie Day Care

The concept: play all day, have great walks and come home happy! Some day cares have pick up and delivery, most take drop off animals. Cost is usually $15 to $20 for the day, and around $10 per half day. Some also provide day care by the hour.

Aldergrove

Birch-Bark Kennels
26436 - 13th Ave.
856-4321
Board dogs and cats and all other pets. Day care. Also do sick care of small pets and geriatric care.

TNT Retrievers Boarding Kennel and Training Facility
Janice Gunn
27624 Watson Rd.
857-9891
Doggy day care and boarding.

Burnaby

Aberdeen Animal Hospital
4856 E. Hastings St.
293-1294
Grooming, full hospital services, boarding, day care. Associated with Fraserview Animal Clinic and Kerrisdale Hospital in Vancouver, amd Aberdeen Kennel and Cattery in Richmond.

Tire Biter Depot, the first dog day care centre in Canada, opened in 1992 in Toronto. This is turning out to be a very popular new business idea.

Bowser and Co.
390 Howard Ave
299-6434
U-wash centre, full service grooming, doggy day care.

Burnaby Veterinary Hospital
2210 Springer
299-0688
Day care and boarding.

Kidd Kare Pet Services
329-3736
Pet taxi, day care, dogwalking and kennel-free boarding.

Delta

Studio One
5669 - 12th Ave.
Tsawwassen
943-7812
Small and medium breeds, grooming, day care during business hours.

Delta Kennels
4335 - 104th St.
596-0911

Ladner

On The Spot Pet Grooming
5040 - 48th Ave.
940-0009
Day care, self-serve dogwash, pet boutique and giftshop.

New Westminster

Tiffany's Doggy Salon
29 - 8th Ave.
526-5026
Up to three walks a day, plus grooming.

Port Coquitlam

Countryside Kennels
558 Prairie Ave.
945-0125
Day care, grooming, obedience training.

Kendon Kennels
1185 Dominion
941-2313
Day care and boarding kennel.

Richmond

Aberdeen Kennel & Cattery Ltd.
7300 No. 5 Rd.
273-3022
Day care, boarding kennels and grooming.

Alabon Country Kennels
20391 Westminster Hwy.
270-2822
Day care, boarding kennels and grooming.

Kidd Kare Pet Services
329-3736
Pick-up and delivery, walks to beach and parks, boarding (kennel free) and pet taxi.

Pads and Paws Pet Motel
6151 No. 7 Rd.
273-8177
Day care and boarding.

Pampering Pets
7866 Williams Ave.
241-0130
Day care by the hour.

The Pampered Pooch
6120 No. 5 Rd.
279-1525
Has 2.5 acres of land and 1250 square-foot shed with chesterfields and chairs to play on. All dogs welcome. Open Monday to Friday, 7 a.m. to 6:30 p.m.; $20 per day.

Penny's Dog Grooming
2 - 8671 No. 1 Rd.
272-5095
Day care by the hour.

Perfect Pet Care
Deborah Wolfe
878-0364
Pet sitting, training, walking, day care.

Rondivills
16640 Westminster Hwy.
278-7181
Training, boarding, day care, grooming, pet taxi.

Dawgs & Katz
9478 - 120 St.
581-1646
Do-it-yourself dogwash, day care by the day.

Meadow View Acres
Bonnie/ Moe Ritch
4044 - 184th St.
574-2323
Grooming, training, boarding.

North American Guard Dog & Kenneling Services Ltd.
16238 - 56th Ave.
574-9757
Grooming, training, behaviour modification, training of dog trainers, kennels.

Vancouver
The Doghouse
105 - 1833 Anderson St. (entrance to Granville Island)
737-7500
Owners drop off and pick up. On a half-day/daily basis, open 6:30 a.m. to 6:30 p.m.

Fraser Pet Hospital
4305 Fraser
872-7671
Day care, grooming, boarding.

Fraserview Animal Clinic
7291 Fraser St.
324-1523
Some grooming. Veterinary care and day care. Connected

Reverend Shelagh MacKinnon takes her dog Beauregard to work at St. Andrew's-Wesley Church. When MacKinnon is counselling people, Beauregard helps reassure them.

with Kerrisdale Veterinary Hospital, Aberdeen Kennel & Cattery (Richmond), Aberdeen Animal Hospital (Burnaby).

Hollywood North Canine Training and Talent Agency
104 - 1037 W. Broadway
738-1568
Day care and training at various levels.

Kerrisdale Veterinary Hospital Ltd.
5999 W. Blvd.
266-4171
Complete hospital facilities, grooming, boarding, day care. Connected with Fraserview Animal Clinic, Aberdeen Kennel & Cattery (Richmond), Aberdeen Animal Hospital (Burnaby).

Kidd Kare Pet Services
329-3736
Pet taxi all over Greater Vancouver area, pick-up and delivery, doggie day care, kennel-free boarding.

Launderdog
1064 Davie St.
685-2306
Full serve and self serve, day care and dogwalking, pet-supplies (Wysong and Koko's natural foods).

Park your Paws Dog Daycare
441 W. 6th Ave.
875-8585
Walking, street safety training, dog massage.

Q. Why do you say Rex is a carpenter dog?

A. Last night, he made a bolt for the door.

Perfect Pet Care
Deborah Wolfe
878-0364
Pet sitting, training, walking.

Point Grey Veterinary Clinic
4362 W. 10th St.
228-1714
Grooming, full veterinary service, shop, training (semi-private and private lessons), boarding, day care, walking.

Vancouver Veterinary Hospital (1991) Ltd.
1541 Kingsway
876-2231
Full veterinary services, day care, boarding.

Yuppy Puppy Dog Day-Care Inc.
1625 W. 3rd St.
732-6446
Day care; also teach outdoor safety training for the dogs.

West Vancouver
Howe Sound Pet Services Ltd.
624 Park Royal North
925-9325
Day care by the hour. Also have a boarding kennel on Bowen Island.

White Rock
White Rock Kennels Ltd.
18867 - 8th Ave.
531-2275
Day care and boarding.

Dave the Canada Post letter carrier has been taking his Border Collie Java to work since she was a puppy. From the early morning stop at the depot, she is showered with affection. Customers who had never spoken to him suddenly opened up and have become great pals of Java.

Bird feeder by
Graham Eagle-Ayrie Studio

THE WORKING DOG

Here are some of the usual — and not so usual — jobs for dogs in the Vancouver area.

Movie Recruitment Companies

Animal Handlers and Trainers

Advanced Trainers
Shawn Myers
33 - 10579 King George Hwy.
Surrey
462-7417
e-mail: administration@animaltrainers.com
Training and supplying dogs for film, video and multi-media productions.

Cinemazoo Animal Agency Ltd.
6939 Hastings St.
Burnaby
299-6963
Animal acting classes, all breeds welcome.

Coe's Animal Talent Inc.
Debra J. Coe
Box 24, 402 - 814 Richards St.
Vancouver
689-7243

Creative Animal Talent Ltd.
Mark Weiner-Dumas and Dawn Dumas
R.R. 3, 36428 Kussman Rd.
Mission
820-1175 or 462-9888
Train and supply animals for the film industry.

Hollywood North Canine Training and Talent Agency
104-1037 W. Broadway
Vancouver
738-1568

Guide Dogs and Assistance Dogs

British Columbia Guide Dog Services (BC GDS)
Bill Thornton
940-4504
BC GDS provides training and guide dogs for the visually impaired. Applicants must be at least 14 years of age. Successful applicants are trained privately in-home, or in a group at the BC GDS facilities. Assistance is provided to graduates when needed. BC GDS primarily uses Labrador Retrievers or Golden Retrievers, and sometimes Standard Poodles and German Shepherds. Dogs are trained by the BC GDS. The organization also runs a puppy foster-care program. Puppies are placed with volunteers for 14 months before they begin guide dog training. Veterinarian and food costs are covered. The BC GDS relies on donations and volunteers.

BC Pets & Friends
Executive Director: Judith McBride
250-167 W. 2nd Ave.
879-5991
Newsletter: *Paws to Reflect*
website: http://www.sns.cs.ubc.ca/jennifer/bcpets.html
BC Pets & Friends coordinate about 400 volunteer teams that visit people who are elderly, chronically ill or disabled in care facilities across the Lower Mainland. Teams are made up of human and animal volunteers. Dogs are the most popular animals, but cats, birds and even rabbits are welcome visitors. Volunteers are asked to visit for at least an hour once a week, for a year. The residents of the care facilities find these visits invaluable, and they are rewarding experiences for the volunteers too. Interaction with animals can improve the quality of life, reduce stress and bring love, affection and friends into the lives of people in care facilities. Research shows that when you are around an animal, you smile more, communicate better and have lower blood pressure. The volunteers and their animals are the only visitors for some people in the care facilities. Residents say having a pet around makes the facility seem less institutional; in some cases, patients who haven't talked for years suddenly find words when they are around an animal.

Anne Fownes puppy-walked Quadra, a Golden Retriever. It was difficult to give her up, but Quadra was bred to work. Eventually Anne met Quadra's new owner, Karen, who is in the middle of a three-year massage therapy course with Quadra by her side. Anne was delighted at the match and at how Quadra has given Karen confidence, mobility and independence.

Volunteers bring their own pets to BC Pets & Friends and the animals are assessed for compatibility and behaviour around people. Successful teams are then trained how to react around elderly or ill people. Teams can visit individuals or groups, and often the host institution will arrange group activities to coincide with the weekly visit. BC Pets & Friends is a non-profit organization that helps bring happiness to about 15,000 people in the Lower Mainland, but there is still a waiting list for teams, and volunteers are always welcome.

Canadian Guide Dogs for the Blind (CGDB), BC

Provincial Coordinator: Denise Berg
241-8828
Puppy Walking Supervisor: Roberta Whiley
594-0641
National Newsletter: *Side by Side*
This branch trains and supports visually impaired people of Western Canada who are obtaining a guide dog. Volunteer puppy walkers foster a puppy for 14 months, then the dog goes for formal training to Manotick, Ontario. Eventually the dogs will be matched up with a client. The CGBD British Columbia headquarters is a residence in Richmond where clients stay for a period to train with their new dog. CGDB is also involved with fund-raising and public awareness. The CGDB annual walk is always the last Sunday in May, in Stanley Park.

Pacific Assistance Dogs Society (PADS)

Executive Director: Laura Watamanuk
527-0556
(formerly Western Canada Handi and Hearing Ear Dogs Society; affiliated with Canine Companions for Independence in the United States)

PADS is a non-profit organization that trains and provides dogs to the physically disabled, the deaf or hearing impaired, and others who may need assistance, like stroke victims and people with Alzheimer's or multiple sclerosis. The dogs are trained to perform tasks such as turning on light switches, carrying packages, retrieving dropped items, or even answering telephones. These special dogs greatly improve the quality of life of their owners.

There is increasing evidence that dogs are extremely therapeutic — especially in long-term-stay hospitals. There are at least five dogs at Vancouver General Hospital that come in on a regular basis. They mostly visit in the long-stay units, where they become old friends with the patients. Mary Blake, a psychologist with the Geriatric Psychiatry Outreach Department takes Maggie, a 12-year-old Border Collie, to work every day. They see patients in their homes and other facilities, travelling by McClure Cabs, where Maggie is honorary mascot for the drivers. Mary says, "Dogs are totally non-judgemental, they don't care about your history, they just give affection."

Since starting their service in 1987, PADS has placed 27 dogs with people who need them. The waiting period to receive a service and social dog is three years; for a hearing dog, the waiting period is one year. Service and social dogs are Labradors or Retrievers and are trained in physical assistance. Hearing dogs are smaller breeds such as Poodles or Shelties and are taught to respond to household sounds. The dogs are donated by breeders, shelters or privately. PADS is always looking for volunteers and dogs. They hold an annual fund-raising dog walk in Langley in mid-summer.

Pat-a-Pup
Penny Lummis or Bonnie Dyck
533-5089 or 857-8998
A casual organization working in Langley, Cloverdale and Abbotsford to complement the activities programs in extended care centres. Every Thursday morning, a group of three to nine dogs and owners visit centres (on a rotational basis). Volunteers are asked to commit to at least one Thursday a month. All dogs must have all current vaccinations, have completed Level One dog (and owner) obedience, and be sociable with strangers and other dogs. Humans who have the gift of gab and a sociable dog have a great time visiting with the residents.

Public Awareness Without Sight (PAWS)
Lori Shepherd
522-9222
Lori Shepherd and her colleagues consult with hotels, restaurants, financial institutions and businesses wanting to enhance their customer service. Her company does menus for the blind and offers disability awareness training. Lori is on the access advisory committee for the city and is an agency speaker for the United Way. With her Yellow Labrador Renee, she coordinated a recent International Guide Dog User Conference.

A friendly female cashier at the Vancouver Transfer Station at Kent Avenue has a cache of dog cookies in her wicket booth for hungry canines.

Vancouver Airport Dogs

If you see Beagles or a Black Labradors walking around the airport next time you fly, don't disturb them — they are working hard. If, however, they come your way and sit next to you, start to worry. These dogs are looking for illegal items being brought into Vancouver from other countries.

The Beagle probably belongs to the Canadian Food Inspection Agency. The agency uses hounds — Beagles and Beagle look-alikes — because they are friendly, non-aggressive dogs and are good trackers. The program started in Vancouver in 1984 and there are currently two dog teams working the international arrivals customs halls, sniffing out the smell of agricultural commodities. They are trained to pick out 50 different smells and can detect birds, plants, meat, dairy products, soil, seeds, fruit, vegetables and bulbs. At certain times of the year, such as tulip season, the smell of tulip bulbs is reinforced with the dogs. Or, if there is an outbreak of a disease like Newcastle, a disease affecting foul, the bird scent is reinforced with the dogs.

The dogs are trained to sit when they find something. If the dog indicates it has found something, Agriculture Canada personnel at the airport will do an inspection. They usually find meat, fruit and dairy products — most of them brought in by people who can't get the same quality in Canada. The declaration card asks specifically for these commodities, and if the importer has marked "no," and the dog indicates "yes," that's a false declaration. Meats, fruits and grains can carry insects and diseases. Compared to the rest of Canada, British Columbia is relatively pest free, and Agriculture Canada wants to keep it that way. So if we grow it, don't bring it in. For now, the seized goods are incinerated and the importer let off, but a ticketing system is in the works.

Customs dogs stats:
The detector dogs at the Vancouver International Airport were responsible for 204 drug seizures, totalling over $2 million, from July 1996 to May 1997.

FIRE HOSE

The Black Labradors at the airport belong to Revenue Canada Customs. The customs agents are looking for narcotics, guns and ammunition, so they prefer to use a bigger, more aggressive dog. Also, Labradors and Retrievers are excellent trackers. The dogs are trained to react in two different ways: actively and passively. Passive dogs sit when they have found something, and active dogs bark and scratch. Because the passive dogs attract less attention, they are used around people in the terminals. The Vancouver Airport Customs Dog Team is just over a year old, but the program has been running in other parts of the country since 1978. Handler Rob Freer says the dogs are just amazing. They don't give up until they find something — one dog even found a packet of hash wrapped in a baggie, then tinfoil, then a cold cream jar placed inside a suitcase. The dogs live with their handlers and when they retire after five to 10 years of work, they are either adopted or stay with the handlers as pets. If these dogs find something, you will most definitely be arrested.

Toronto Dominion Bank manager Elaine Latimore says that the branch on West 57th Avenue welcomes doggie visitors. She knows them all by name, and distributes treats to these customers.

Police Dogs

Vancouver Police Dog Squad

Vancouver's Police Dog Squad has achieved a lot of firsts since it was created in 1957. It is the first municipal police department dog squad in Canada, the first to use female dogs and the first to train dogs as part of an Emergency Response Team. The 17 dog squad teams are split into two platoons which ensure the city is covered 24 hours a day. The dog squad uses German Shepherds because they are easy to train, are big and strong enough for the job, look menacing and are very good trackers. The bigger the nose, the better the tracker — and German Shepherds have very big noses.

The dogs often are used in situations where a suspect has recently left the scene of the crime — for example, robbery, breaking and entering, auto theft, purse snatching and prowling. They are taught to track the scent of the sweat people give off when they are nervous, which is distinctive to each of us and different from general sweat. When the dog apprehends a suspect, it will simply bark if the person is non-aggressive; if the suspect tries

Portrait by
Kristine Kavalec

to run, however, the dog will use whatever force is necessary to hold the person down. Police dogs attended over 12,000 calls last year and were deployed in a large percentage of those calls. That resulted in 289 dog apprehensions and many more assists.

When the police dogs aren't working, they are expected to participate in public relations programs. They visit schools, hospitals and community groups to familiarize the public with their special skills. Although dogs are trained to be aggressive, they are gentle when not working and behave well in public. A police dog lives with its handler and is devoted to its master. After working for eight to 10 years, the dog retires to the handler's home as the family pet.

Vancouver Dog Squad Statistics

- The squad goes through 10,000 pounds of dog food a year.
- Most popular Vancouver Dog Squad Names: Shadow (six to date), Prince (five to date), King (five), Sabre (four). Pop Culture has had an influence on names over the years. Dogs have been called Griff, Saint, Vader, Bronson, Conan, Judge and Justice.
- The Vancouver Dog Squad averages 800 calls a month, and most of those calls are between 10 p.m. and 5 a.m.
- A "quarry" is a pretend bad guy or suspect. The VPD has about 18 to 20 on-call quarries, mostly men aged 16 to 35 who take part in the dog training. They get paid to be bad guys and get chased by dogs.

- The total costs of food, vet care and other expenses for the 17 dogs on the Vancouver Dog Squad is less than keeping one human officer on the road for one year. The Dog Squad used to acquire dogs by donation and they had to screen many dogs in order to find one with potential. The squad has recently begun their own breeding program and have had a terrific success rate.
- Seven dogs have been killed in the line of duty since the Dog Squad was formed in 1957. A memorial plaque with the seven names is displayed in the foyer of the Police Headquarters and honours the following dogs: Valiant, shot; Justin, stabbed; Pax, fell seven stories; Conan, Bobby, Mecca, hit by car; and Sabre, involved in squad car accident.

North Vancouver RCMP Police Dog Service Section

This information on the RCMP's Police Dog Service Section is reprinted from their website (http://www.district.north-van.bc.ca/home/psd.html).

The majority of our dogs are German Shepherds, but there are a number of Belgian Malinois being used as well. The handlers and dogs are trained for a variety of duties, including searching for lost persons and property, drug detection and apprehension of criminals. We have two specially trained dog/handler teams for explosives detection, and mountain and avalanche search and rescue duties. One team is trained in Emergency Response Team tactics and operations, and riot and crowd control. Each team responds to approximately 600 calls for service per year. Teams work in all types of weather and terrain — it's a physically demanding job for both dog and handler.

Vancouver Business Dogs

They say that having a dog around decreases your stress level, to say nothing of getting you out for a walk. Having a dog in the office also makes for a better working environment, and it is said to make people feel more comfortable in a retail situation — the dog as icebreaker. The chatting that ensues has even been known to increase sales. In the lower mainland there are many many folks

Women in Print Books on 4th Avenue has a "Dog Wall of Fame." Polaroid photos are taken of regular doggie visitors and posted on the store's bulletin board. Louise and Carol have an ample supply of biscuits and the occasional tennis ball for their four-legged customers.

who take their dogs to work. Here's a smattering of the more public working dogs.

- Abbie and Shane the Bouviers, who go to work with Yvonne Savard at the Vancouver Regional Branch of the SPCA.
- Abraham the Border Collie Shepherd mix, at Kama on 4th Avenue.
- Benny the Border Collie X, at Storm Hairdressers on Robson.
- Caspin and Rilian the Miniature Black Poodles, at Damask Designs on 4th Avenue.
- Gracie the Border Collie and Coda the Black Lab, at Dig This on Granville Island.
- Iceberg the Pug, at Once Again on 1st Avenue.
- Mr. Flint the Boxer, at the Steveston Barber Shop.
- Nicholas the King Charles Cavalier Spaniel, at Portabello Antiques on Granville Stree.
- Sheba the Doberman guard dog, at Ragnar's Jewellry on Granville Street.
- Spot the Malti-poo Terrier X, at Petley-Jones Gallery on Granville Street.
- Sultan the Black Standard Poodle, at Straith's in the Hotel Vancouver.
- Taxi the Golden Retriever, Jack the Yellow Labrador and Pablo the Malti-poo at Diane Farris Gallery, 7th Avenue and Granville Street.
- Titan the Rotweiller Lab X, at Remax at Oakridge.
- Tosca the Golden Retriever, at Europe Bound on Dunsmuir Avenue.

VII. Kids & Dogs

Who knew? Vancouver is not only Dog City — it's Kids-and-Dogs City, too. This didn't start out as a chapter on its own, but I'm delighted to have discovered enough information about children and dogs in the Lower Mainland to create a separate section. There are a number of agencies to be commended for their children's education programs, including the British Columbia SPCA and its various branches, FIDO, the Junior Kennel Clubs and the 4H. A solid grounding in responsible dog ownership and in how to approach and handle dogs can only make for a better lifelong relationship with everybody's "best friend."

EVERY KID'S DOG CARE GUIDE

— *British Columbia SPCA*

Friends for Life

Animals trust you to provide care for the rest of their lives. This is a big responsibility but it is very rewarding. Here is what you must provide for your pet:

Food: All animals need to be fed the correct food. Cats cannot eat dog food, guinea pigs cannot eat rabbit pellets and birds cannot live on seeds alone. Generally, if your pets are young and active, they need high energy food. When they get older and slow down they need food that has less fat.

Water: Give your pet plenty of fresh water. While there are many different types of animals, one thing they have in common is that they all require fresh water. Change the water every day and wash the water container regularly.

Shelter: Shelters should keep your pet warm, dry and safe. Dogs need a weatherproof dog house.

Exercise: Keep your pet fit. Walk your dog twice a day — plenty of exercise will keep your dog happy and healthy.

Little tiny puppy dog
Sleeping soundly like a log
Better wake him for his
dinner
Or else he'll start to sleep
much thinner.
— Spike Milligan

Vet Care: All animals should be taken to a veterinarian for regular checkups. Your veterinarian will give you advice on a proper diet for your dog, help your dog if it becomes sick, and will give the proper vaccinations your dog may need to prevent diseases. The vet will also spay or neuter your dog and can even provide an identification tattoo or microchip in case your dog gets lost.

Grooming: Dogs need regular brushing to keep their coats soft and tangle-free. Grooming your dog is also a good way of looking for health problems such as itchy skin, fleas or other bumps. Dogs also need to be bathed now and then and should have their nails clipped occassionally. This is a job for your veterinarian or a parent.

Friendship: All dogs need a best friend — someone who will spend time with them and take care of them for the rest of their lives. That's YOU!

Q: What's happening when you hear "Woof! ...Splat ...Meow! ...Splat"?

A: It's raining cats and dogs.

Dog bowl by
Georgina Brandon

SAFETY TIPS

Things to Remember About Dogs

British Columbia SPCA, Bite Free Program
- Ask permission before petting someone else's dog.
- Leave mother animals and their young alone.
- Do not try to pet dogs that are tied up, sleeping, eating, behind fences, or in vehicles.
- Do not tease, chase, or yell at dogs.
- Do not pull their ears or tails.
- Do not grab their food, bones or toys.
- Do not try to stop a fight. Call an adult for help.
- Always act kindly and gently. Animals have feelings too.
- Leave wild animals alone.
- Report the details of injured, stray and threatening animals to an adult, who will call the SPCA or animal control authorities.

How to Act Around a Stray Dog
- Do not pet strays.
- Stand still (stand like a tree!).
- Let the dog sniff you.
- Do not stare at the dog. Dogs view this as aggressive behaviour. Turn your head to the side.
- Do not turn your back and run.
- If the dog is barking or growling, slowly walk away, backwards or sideways, keeping the dog in view.
- If the dog bites or jumps on you, lie face down and cover the back of your neck (lie like a log!).
- Be as still and quiet as possible (stand like a tree!).

"Outside of a dog, a book is a man's best friend. Inside of a dog, it's too dark to read."
— Groucho Marx

214

YOUTH PROGRAMS

The Animal Learning Centre

The Animal Learning Centre at the SPCA in Surrey is unique in North America. As well as being a resource centre for children and a club house, it is a place where school classes can come for workshops throughout the school year. For more information, call the SPCA Youth Program at 594-PAWS.

SPCA Youth Club

Kids and dogs are a natural mix — and through the SPCA there are ample opportunities for animal encounters. Members of the SPCA Youth Club (which includes approximately 700 kids between the ages of six and 15 in the Lower Mainland) can participate in all sorts of animal activities:

- Volunteering in the shelters in Vancouver and Surrey. At first, children work mainly with cats, small animals and farm animals (mostly in Surrey). This gives them the experience they need to help with the dogs.
- Learning to groom and train dogs. This activity takes place in Surrey at the new Animal Learning Centre.
- Being a representative of the SPCA at school. Children can organize a visit from the SPCA to their school. This promotes the SPCA youth programs.
- Helping to produce the newsletter, *Paws for Thought*. Kids help with writing, editing, cartoons and photography.
- Fund raising for the SPCA

For more information, call the SPCA Youth Program at 594-PAWS.

SPCA Summer Camp

All young people in the Lower Mainland between six and 12 years old can attend SPCA summer day camps. For information, call Natasha at 594-PAWS.

> "The dog was created especially for children. He is the god of frolic."
> — Henry Ward Beecher

SPCA Program for School Classes

Instructors will come to the classroom, or classes can visit to the Animal Learning Centre in Surrey (for information, call 594-PAWS). The SPCA has the following programs for school classes in the Lower Mainland:
- Bite Free
- Companion Animal Care
- Respect for Animals
- Animal Abuse and How You Can Prevent It (for Grades 7 onwards)
- Urban Wildlife

SPCA Junior Pet Show

The SPCA has a Junior Pet Show each year (they celebrate their 50th Annual show in 2001!). Call for information on time and place: 594-PAWS.

CLUBS

4H Clubs

For general information on 4H clubs in the Lower Mainland, call:
Pat Tonn
Youth Development Specialist, Ministry of Agriculture
Abbotsford
556-3067

Langley
K-9 4H Dog Club
Joanne White
Langley
856-6876
For ages nine to 19. Public speaking, demonstrations, training and showing — participants must keep record books on their dog. Holds a dog show put on by the kids.

Mother: Can I have a puppy for my son?

Pet store owner: Sorry ma'am, we don't do swaps.

Maple Ridge
Kanaka 4H Horse and Dog Club
Birgitte Knudsen
Maple Ridge
467-6257
Dog training and showing. Kids aged nine to 20.
Two meetings a month.

Mission
North Fraser Dog 4H Club
Margaret Krieck
Mission
826-1968 or 826-4496

Surrey
Countryside 4H Horse and Dog Club
Colleen Marlikowski
Surrey
541-1287

Kennel Clubs

Junior Kennel Club Of Vancouver
Marion Postgate or Mary Jay Douglas
263-9082 or 274-3318
Active since 1953, this club welcomes 10 to 19 year olds
and all kinds of dogs. Members train for fun and/or
competition. The club offers instruction in show handling
and/or obedience training, plus information on dogs.
Meetings are held on Saturdays from 12 p.m. to 3 p.m.
at Sidaway School, Richmond. An eight-week course costs
$30.

Lower Mainland Junior Kennel Club of British Columbia, Surrey chapter
Lea Oiom
Surrey
588-0280
Welcomes children from five to 17 years of age. Teaches
them to train dogs for obedience and/or show ring.
Hopes to have an obedience obstacle course by next year.
Activities throughout the year including an annual field
trip to a dog show. Members don't have to own a dog.

Two fleas are coming out of the movies, and it's raining very hard outside. One flea says to the other, "What are we going to do? Should we walk or wait for a dog?"

DOGS IN THE CLASSROOM

Humane Education

— Stephen Huddart, Education Director, BC SPCA

Seymour, a dignified older dog, comes to class regularly with his best friend, a Grade Five teacher at Tecumseh Elementary named Alex Angelomatis ("Mr. A" to his pupils). "Just by being in the classroom, Seymour acts as a catalyst for participation — shy kids get involved, listening improves, and the class gets along better...from the changes I've seen, every class should have an animal for students to relate to and care for," says Mr. A.

Harvard biologist E.O. Wilson has termed the phenomena Mr. A describes as *biophilia* — simply, "the innate tendency to focus on life." In his landmark 1984 book by that name, Wilson suggested that the evolutionary history of human thought, language and socialization has been profoundly influenced by our species' relationships with other animals. But animals teaching people — can this have implications for learning today?

In a book called *Biophilia Hypothesis* (Island Press, 1993) researchers Katcher and Wilkins surveyed several studies involving children, animals and education. Among their conclusions:

1. Animals brought into a human context are powerful reinforcers of human attention and behaviour.
2. When a child is given the opportunity to interact with an animal as well as watch it, there are more positive changes in behaviour and they are more persistent.
3. Human speech and the nonverbal expression of emotion are facilitated by the presence of animals.

When students work together to take care of an animal in the classroom, the resulting ethic of cooperation and caring extends naturally to other children, and to the world outside the classroom. Humane education, while focussing on the human/animal relationship, provides a lens through which environmental issues, personal health and safety, and cooperative learning can be brought into sharper focus.

Mr. A's story is turning out to be an unhappy one. The school board has intervened and banned dogs from schools because a parent expressed concern about possible bites or allergies. Four hundred kids created a 700-name petition to bring back the dog. YTV's *SuperDave* show did a national item, naming Mr. A "hero of the week." But the dog still can't go to school. It stays in the car and visits at recess and lunch hour. There is hope that things will change again soon.

Tom Harder, a continuing education biology teacher in Maple Ridge, and school program coordinator for the BC Humane Education Society (BCHES), has introduced animals and taught the principles of their care to students in more than 150 schools. The following comments are typical of those he receives from teachers:

"Students [learned] about cooperation and sharing of care tasks, responsibility, when [it was] their turn to bring food, and respect for animals and their rights."

"Benefit to students: gentleness, responsibility and new knowledge. Good way to show love and emotion, especially for kids who have behavioural problems and cannot express themselves."

Steve Koebel, now a principal at Maple Elementary, Campbell River, usually had animals in his class, and noticed that, years later, students' memories seemed clearly linked to the presence of those animals. Curiosity about memory creation led him to research and write a comprehensive paper on the role of animals in education, "Animals, Children, and Related School Board Policy in the Elementary School." In it he finds ample evidence that the "biophilia factor" strongly enhances learning situations. He also examines practical and ethical concerns about keeping animals in classrooms. In calling

Q: What is the difference between a good dog and a bad student?

A: One rarely bites, the other barely writes.

Photograph by
Yukiko Onley

for the creation of school board policy on animals in the classroom, he writes, "...teachers need to be encouraged to enable their students to be in contact with animals and they need to know the School Board supports this...[but] certain guidelines for animal care, maintenance and safety must be observed and regulated." Koebel concludes his paper with a useful set of guidelines designed to assist trustees and senior management in developing such a policy.

In society's continuing and critical search for paths to a peaceful, sustainable future, humane education and the biophilia hypothesis open up some very promising possibilities. The BC SPCA Education Division is working with school boards, administrators, teachers, students and the animal welfare community to develop policies and programs that reflect and support our evolving relationships with animals.

SPCA Adopt a Kennel Program

In the Lower Mainland, kids in classrooms are helping unwanted cats and dogs by sponsoring care of the animals at their local SPCA. How can your class get involved?

A school or classroom can sponsor a kennel at its local shelter by having each student donate one loonie a month to support an animal. In return, your class photograph will be displayed on the kennel. Also, classes can arrange for a tour of the shelter. If the kennel becomes vacant, the money will be used to help sick and injured animals at the Vancouver SPCA Animal Clinic.

If you wish to participate in the Kennel Program or require more information, contact:
SPCA Youth Program
Adopt a Kennel
1205 E. 7th Ave.
Vancouver
V5T 1R1
263-4963 or 323-2775
Fax: 263-4918

Bob Gordon, Director of Shelter Operations at the Vancouver Regional Branch of the SPCA, started as a volunteer when he was 14 years old. He has been working at the SPCA for 31 years.

RESOURCES FOR KIDS

Videos

Bite Free: Playing It Safe With Dogs
This video, aimed at children between four and 10 years old, is an amusing look at dog bite prevention from the dog's point of view. Included is a dog-bite safety brochure for parents and a fold-out board game for kids. The video costs $24.95 and can be ordered by calling 683-7697 or 1-800-665-6636.

Books

Vancouver Kidsbooks' Best Dog Books for Children:

Picture Books
Martha Speaks, by Susan Meddaugh (Houghton Mifflin)
The Night I Followed the Dog, by Nina Laden (Chronicle Books)
My Dog Rosie, by Isabelle Harper and Barry Moser (Blue Sky Press/Scholastic)
McDuff Comes Home, by Rosemary Wells and Susan Jeffers (Hyperion)
How Smudge Came, by Nan Gregory and Ron Lightburn (Red Deer College Press)
Mary of Mile 18, by Ann Blades (Tundra Books)

Novels
Shiloh, by Phyllis Reynolds Naylor (Collier Macmillan Canada)
The Trouble with Tuck, by Theodore Taylor (Doubleday)
Where the Redfern Grows, by Wilson Rawls (Doubleday)
The Dog Who Wouldn't Be, by Farley Mowat (Seal Books)
James Herriot's Dog Stories, by James Herriot (M. Joseph)

Q: What is the difference between a flea-bitten dog and a bored student?

A: One is going to itch, the other is itching to go.

FURTHER RESOURCES

Dogs on the Internet

On the Venn Diagram of dog-people and folks on the internet, there is a huge overlap. And no wonder! The Internet is a great resource for everything from breed information to treatments for hip dysplasia to dog-show times and dates, and much more. It is also an excellent way to "network" with others interested in breed rescue, or to trace tattoos of lost dogs. Here are the "raw bones" on how you and your dog can begin surfing:

E-mail Lists

As well as newsgroups and web sites, a feature of the internet is the ability to subscribe to a topical list which deposits the discussion into your e-mail slot. For a massive list of these dog forums, consult this website: http://www.zmall.com/pet_talk/pet-faqs/dog-faqs/lists/email-list.html

The Big Lists:
Canadian Pet Sites Index
website: http://www.interlog.com/~pets/cpsidir.html
A list of Canadian dog-related links that include the Canadian Veterinary Medicine Association, the Pacific Animal Therapy Society (PATS) and the Pet Loss Support Line.

Compupets
website: http://www.compupets.com/
A Vancouver-based pet information source with a breeder directory, classified ads, dog shows and events, dog goods, training information and much more.

Electronic Zoo/Net Vet
website: http://netvet.wustl.edu/dogs.htm
An incredibly comprehensive list of links to breed information and hot dog topics.

Informational Dog-related Web Sites
website: http://www.zmall.com/pet_talk/dog-faqs/lists/www-list.html

FAQS
website: http://www.zmall.com/pet_talk/pet-faqs/
Rec.pet.dogs is one of the most active newsgroups on the internet. A master lister, Cindy Tittle Moore, has compiled FAQS (Frequently Asked Questions) from the forum into a website where you will find information on all aspects of dog ownership.

Newsgroups
These are some of my favourite dog newsgroups.
- rec.hunting.dogs
- rec.pets.dogs
- rec.pets.dogs.activities
- rec.pets.dogs.behavior
- rec.pets.dogs.breeds
- rec.pets.dogs.health
- rec.pets.dogs.info
- rec.pets.dogs.misc

On-line Canadian Dog Magazines
Canine Review
website: http://kamloops.netshop.net/caninerev/

Dogs in Canada
website: http://www.dogs-in-canada.com/

Top Dogs Magazine
website: http://www.execulink.com/~topdogs/

Websites on Humane and Environmental Education:
American SPCA (ASPCA)
website: http://www.aspca.org/
Lists teacher resources and programs available.

Animal Behaviour and Welfare Sites
website: http://www.wam.umd.edu/~jaguar/

BC SPCA
website: http://www.bcyellowpages.com/BCHES/

Canadian Federation of Humane Societies
website: http://infoweb.magi.com/~cfhs/

Environmental Education
website: http://eelink.umich.edu

Humane Society of the US (HSUS)
website: http://www.hsus.org
Has brochure samples and lists of materials to order.

Magazines

Pacific Cats & Dogs
(formerly Paws Magazine)
circulation: Vancouver-based; province-wide

Rescue: BC SPCA Animal Care and Protection
681-7271
e-mail: bcspca@mindlink.bc.ca

Newspapers

Langley Advance News
"Dog Tales"
Vicky O'Connor, columnist
Column appears every Friday. Covers some dog behaviour and safety issues, equipment, responsible dog ownership. Geared towards common-sense education of pet owners.

The Pet Gazette
534-6966 or 826-1606
A free pet ad paper distributed throughout the Lower Mainland.

The Province
Deborah Wolfe, Pet Therapist
Advice column appears each Sunday in the "Take a Break" section. Wolfe, author of *Good Dog! Positive Dog Training Techniques* (Polestar Book Publishers), is a trainer and the owner of Perfect Pet Care, which offers training, walking and doggie day-care.

Vancouver Sun
Nicholas Read, columnist
Column on animal issues appears each Tuesday. Read is the author of *One in a Million* (Polestar Book Publishers), a story about a dog in an animal shelter, for children between the ages of 7 and 11.

Radio

CKNW
"Bill Good Show"
Veterinarinan Dr. Joel Parker is a frequent guest on the Bill Good Show.

CKST
"Pet Chat"
Hosted by Dr. James Anthony. Thursday mornings, 11:30 a.m. to noon.

KISS-FM
Nicholas Read appears on Tuesday mornings with hosts Fred and Cathy.

Television

All About Pets
Ainslie Mills appears live on the second Friday of the month, at 8 p.m., on Rogers' Community Television Cable throughout Lower Mainland. The show repeats on the third Friday of the month at 8 p.m. Sponsored by FIDO.

BCTV Noon News
Eileen Drever of the Surrey SPCA does a weekly spot on animals available for adoption.

Critter's Corner
Burnaby SPCA's Hugh Nichols appears on the first and third Tuesdays of each month at 7:30 p.m. on Rogers' Community Cable in Burnaby.

Pet Talk
Vancouver SPCA's Bob Gordon appears on Roger's Cable on the fourth Friday of the month at 8 p.m.

Today at the SPCA
Delta SPCA's Shawn Eccles appears on Delta Cable throughout the week: Mondays at 5:30 p.m., Tuesdays at 10 p.m., Wednesday 6:30 p.m., Thursdays at 10 p.m., Fridays at 7:30 p.m., Sundays at 10 p.m.

Miscellaneous

Talking Yellow Pages
(299) 900-9770
Has consumer tips on choosing a pet, things to consider before you buy, pet first aid, fitness and nutrition.

Vancouver Public Library
There are 699 books under the subject of "Dogs in Fiction" at the Vancouver Public Library. Check'em out.

CREDITS & CONTRIBUTORS

I. Finding Your Dog

"Things to Consider About Adopting a Dog" reprinted with permission from the BC SPCA.

"Where to Look" reprinted, with permission, from the Canadian Veterinary Medical Association publication, "A Commonsense Guide to Selecting a Dog or a Cat."

"Breeds Recognized by the Canadian Kennel Club" reprinted courtesy of *Dogs in Canada* magazine.

"What is FIDO?" reprinted with permission of FIDO.

Part II. Good Dog Owner Etiquette

"Are you a Responsible Dog Owner?" reprinted with permission from FIDO.

"Dogs and the Law" reprinted with the permission of the Canadian Bar Association, BC Branch, from Dial-A-Law tape 640. Dial-a-Law (c) is funded by the Law Foundation of British Columbia, and is sponsored by the BC Branch of the Canadian Bar Association.

"Animal Control By-laws in Vancouver" reprinted with the permission of the City of Vancouver.

"Liability Insurance for Dog Owners," by Mike Grenby, reprinted with the permission of the author.

"Leash it or Lose It" reprinted with the permission of the Greater Vancouver Regional District (GVRD).

"This is a Leash" reprinted with the permission of FIDO.

"Against Tethering" reprinted with the permission of the BC SPCA.

"The Facts of Life" reprinted with the permission of the BC SPCA.

"Dogged by Messy Garbage," by Doug Sagi, reprinted with permission from the *Vancouver Sun* (Saturday, June 23, 1990).

"The Urban Coyote Project," by Kristine Webber, reprinted with permission from the author and the Urban Wildlife Committee.

"Finding Your Lost Dog" and "ID Your Dog" reprinted with the permission of the BC SPCA.

III. Caring For Your Dog

"Beautifying Your Beast" reprinted with the permission of the Western Professional Dog Groomer's Association.

IV. Walking Your Dog

Parts of "Dog Walks in the Lower Mainland" reprinted with permission from pamphlets and information published by: Burnaby Parks Department; Greater Vancouver Regional District; District and City of North Vancouver ("Dogs in Parks Regulations"); City of Richmond, Community Services ("Discover Richmond Trails"); and District of West Vancouver ("Dog Regulations").

"We're Hunting Wabbits," by Bill Richardson, reprinted with permission of the author.

V. Training & Competing With Your Dog

"The Benefits of a Trained Dog" reprinted with the permission of FIDO.

"Conformation Competition Levels" reprinted with permission from *Dogs in Canada* magazine.

"Lure Coursing" reprinted with the permission of the Canadian Sighthound Field Association.

"Agility" reprinted with the permission of the Agility Association of Canada.

"Flyball," by Ian Hoggs, reprinted with the permission of the author.

"The Schutzhund: A Capable Dog" reprinted with the permission of the German Shepherd Schutzhund Club of Canada.

"Musical Freestyle" reprinted with the permission of Musical Canine Sports International.

VI. Housing, Travelling & Working With Your Dog

"Rental Accommodation," by Stephen Huddart, reprinted with the permission of the BC SPCA.

"The Condo Act," by Margaret Fairweather and Lynn Ramsay, reprinted with permission from *Condominium Law and Practice in British Columbia, 1996.*

"Tips for People Seeking Rental Accomodation," suggested by the Regina Humane Society and

reprinted with permission from *The Voice of Animals* (Fall 1995, Vol. 24, p. 2.)
"North Vancouver RCMP Police Dog Service Section" reprinted from their website at:
http://www.district.north.bc.ca/home/psd.html

VII. Kids & Dogs

"Every Kid's Dog Care Guide" reprinted with the permission of the BC SPCA.
"Things to Remember About Dogs" reprinted with the permission of the BC SPCA.
"Humane Education," by Stephen Huddart, reprinted with the permission of the author.

INDIVIDUAL CONTRIBUTORS

Dr. Stanley Coren is Professor of Psychology at the University of British Columbia, author of *The Intelligence of Dogs* (Free Press, 1994), and a volunteer trainer with the Vancouver Dog Obedience Training Club. He is also the owner of Wiz, a Cavalier King Charles Spaniel and conformation champion with a CDX degree in obedience; and Odin, a large, black, Flat-coated Retriever puppy working on the world's record for the most human faces ever kissed by a dog.

Mike Grenby is an independent advisor who provides financial counseling to individuals and groups. Based in West Vancouver, he has spoken to more than 50,000 people at his annual money shows, writes an award-winning personal finance column and is the author of five books. He and wife Mandy own a Jack Russell Terrier named Sprog that, despite thinking it is a big dog, hasn't been the subject of any dog damage liability suits...yet.

Stephen Huddart is the director of Education and Community Relations for the BC SPCA.

Margot Kerr is a consultant in non-profit management and an aspiring freelance writer.

Marion Postgate is a trainer and obedience judge in the Lower Mainland.

Kristine Webber is the coordinator of the Urban Coyote Project. She gives community talks and advice on coyotes. She can be reached through e-mail at: kwebber@unixg.ubc.ca. She can also be contacted through the BC SPCA or the Urban Wildlife Committee.

Bill Richardson is a CBC radio and television host, and widely read and loved author. Among other distinctions, he is a recipient of the Stephen Leacock Award for Humour. His latest book is *Scorned & Beloved: Dead of Winter Meetings with Canadian Eccentrics* (Knopf Canada). Bill and Smoke live in Vancouver.

Photograph by
Lionel Trudel

Marg Meikle is a freelance researcher, writer and broadcaster who is best-known as the "Answer Lady" on CBC Radio's *Gabereau Show*. Marg contributes to many magazines, has been a syndicated Internet columnist and has written three books: *Dear Answer Lady*, *The Return of the Answer Lady* (both published by Douglas and McIntyre) and *Bumbering Around Vancouver* (Whitecap). In previous lives, Marg earned degrees in Home Economics and Anthropology. She lives in Kitsilano with her husband Noel, Border Collie Rosie and their baby (due in December, 1997).

Please let Marg know about any omissions, additions, deletions or comments for the next edition of *Dog City: Vancouver*. Write to her at:
Marg Meikle
c/o Polestar Book Publishers
P.O. Box 5238, Station B
Victoria, BC
V8R 6N4

Or contact Marg directly:
fax: (604) 736-7052
e-mail: mmeikle@rogers.wave.ca
web page: http://home.bc.rogers.wave.ca/mmeikle

The City Series
Definitive Guides to Your Favourite Pastimes in Your Favourite Cities

The City Series presents a dynamic new way of experiencing favourite cities. These comprehensive guides are written by well-known local experts and include everything you need to know — and more — about popular urban pastimes. Here is trustworthy, indispensable and intriguing information for dog owners, gardeners, outdoor enthusiasts, kids, parents — real people who live, work and play in and around cities. Explore the metropolis in your own way: follow your dog's lead with *Dog City*; grow a green thumb with *Garden City*; hike, bike, climb and work up a sweat with *Active City*; remain young with *Kid City*. The City Series: discovering new worlds in your own backyard.

Watch for:
Garden City: Vancouver
The Definitive Guide for Gardeners in Vancouver and the Lower Mainland

Dog City: Toronto
The Definitive Guide for Dog Owners in Toronto

Sirius Books
An Imprint of Polestar Book Publishers

"Sirius" is the name of the most dominant star in the constellation Canis Major. Also known as the Dog Star, Sirius is the brightest star in the night sky. Sirius Books: A brilliant collection of books for dog lovers.

Non-fiction:
Good Dog! Positive Dog Training Techniques
Deborah Wolfe
1-896095-17-8 • $16.95 CAN • $14.95 USA
A concise and practical guide to basic dog-training commands and techniques.

Young Adult Fiction:
One in a Million
Nicholas Read
1-896095-22-4 • $8.95 CAN • $6.95 USA • ages 8 and up
The story of a dog named Joey, from his days in an animal shelter to his joyous adoption.

DogStar
Beverley Wood & Chris Wood
1-896095-37-2 • $8.95 CAN • $6.95 USA • ages 11 and up
Jeff, a '90s teen, finds himself transported to 1930s Alaska, accompanied by a Bull Terrier named Patsy Ann. Jeff soon discovers that all is not right on the Alaskan frontier. But what can he do to help?
Check out the Patsy Ann website: http://home.istar.ca/~bever/patsyann.htm

---

Polestar Book Publishers
P.O. Box 5238, Station B
Victoria, British Columbia
Canada   V8R 6N4